On Teaching
Foreign Languages

ON TEACHING FOREIGN LANGUAGES

Linking Theory to Practice

MARCELA T. RUIZ-FUNES

CONTEMPORARY LANGUAGE EDUCATION
Terry A. Osborn, Series Adviser

BERGIN & GARVEY
Westport, Connecticut • London

Library of Congress Cataloging-in-Publication Data

Ruiz-Funes, Marcela, 1961–
    On teaching foreign languages : linking theory to practice / Marcela T. Ruiz-Funes.
      p. cm. (Contemporary language education, ISSN 1531–1449)
    Includes bibliographical references and index.
    ISBN 0–89789–785–4 (alk. paper)
    1. Language and languages—Study and teaching—United States. 2. Language
teachers—Training of—United States. I. Title. II. Series.
LB1580.U6R85 2002
418'.0071'173—dc21   2001052794

British Library Cataloguing in Publication Data is available.

Library of Congress Catalog Card Number: 2001052794
ISBN: 0–89789–785–4
ISSN: 1531–1449

First published in 2002

Bergin & Garvey, 88 Post Road West, Westport, CT 06881
An imprint of Greenwood Publishing Group, Inc.
www.greenwood.com

Printed in the United States of America

The paper used in this book complies with the
Permanent Paper Standard issued by the National
Information Standards Organization (Z39.48–1984).

10 9 8 7 6 5 4 3 2 1

To my husband, Gustavo,
My daughters, María and Sofía,
My parents, Hugo and Tere

Contents

Preface

This book addresses a number of salient issues related to foreign language (FL) teaching, learning, and acquisition. Its ultimate goal is to help prospective FL teachers understand the theories and practices in FL education while making such connection more accessible. The selection of topics has been made considering primarily their relevance in the learning-acquisition process of second language (L2) learners and the challenge they pose to beginning FL teachers and interns (student-teachers). This book is the result of a year-long research project conducted during 1999–2000 at East Carolina University, Greenville, North Carolina, in collaboration with four experienced FL high school teachers from the same region. This project was funded by the Schools' Partnership Grant and the BellSouth Foundation.

The main contribution of this book to the FL profession is the integration of the theoretical and practical planes. Both the knowledge of researchers and the voices of experienced FL teachers are brought together. This link aims at helping ease the tension that beginning teachers and interns experience when they move from the FL methods course into the real FL classroom. This connection, in turn, will provide FL interns with a realistic view of FL education.

Four experienced FL teachers from eastern North Carolina participated in this project and discussed their beliefs and experiences in relation to the following theoretical issues: the proficiency movement, the role of input, teaching language in context, class participation, motivation, and discipline. Both a review of the theories and an analysis of the teachers' beliefs are included.

Acknowledgments

I am deeply thankful for the opportunity I was given to work on this project. Professionally, it has been one of the most rewarding experiences as it has helped me gain further insight not only into central issues in foreign language acquisition, learning, and teaching, but also into the role of foreign language education in the United States.

I would like to express my gratitude to the Partnership Grant and BellSouth Foundation of East Carolina University for funding this project. Without their support, I would have not been able to engage in this exploration. In particular, I would like to thank Jon Pederson for his guidance and encouragement throughout the realization of this project.

My warmest appreciation goes to the four expert foreign language teachers who participated in this study—Sandra Stinson and Silvia Briley from J. H. Rose High School, Greenville, North Carolina, and Cathy Moore and Bill Gore from Washington High School, Washington, North Carolina. Their dedication, openness, and energy made this a successful learning experience. I want to thank each of you wholeheartedly.

I am also deeply thankful to a number of people who had faith in this work and gave me the support I needed. I would like to applaud Terry A. Osborn for his approval and guidance; Jane Garry and Liz Leiba for their help as editors; Sylvie Henning and Michael Bassman for their input and recommendations; Brandie Smith, Andrea Conrad, and Jennifer Bannon for their assistance transcribing the video tapes; Judith Shrum for her mentoring throughout my career; my students for their enthusiasm and dedication; and last but not least, my husband, Gustavo; my two daughters, María and Sofia; my parents, Hugo and Tere; my sister,

Mónica, and her family; my bothers, Guillermo y Hugo, and their families; my in-laws, Vilma, Omar, Javier, and Norys and her family; and my friends in Argentina and the United States for their unconditional love.

On Teaching
Foreign Languages

1

Foreign Language Teacher Education: Reflecting on Current Practices

Foreign language teacher education programs in the United States have often been placed in difficult positions between colleges of arts and sciences and schools of education. These programs have been the target of criticism by those who are apprehensive in recognizing their value and treat anything that is related to education as "second-class citizens in today's academy," according to M. H. Long. He continues:

> Those of us in Foreign Language departments who work in or collaborate with Schools of Education on FL teacher preparation are aware of this stereotype. Pervasive snobbery continues in FL departments, where some professors teach literature and others teach language, second language acquisition, and pedagogy. (Long, 2000, p. 434)

Some, such as the former governor of New Jersey, Thomas Kean, have even proposed to do away with courses in education and instead to "select the best and brightest of the students in colleges and universities, make sure that they are well prepared in their major field, and place them in schools with highly competent cooperating teachers for a year of field experience" (Sullivan, 1983 in Wing, 1993). Kean's proposal alarmed FL teachers and teacher educators who claimed that teachers need "academic as well as clinical preparation in how to teach" (Wing, 1993, p. 160). This combination is required because of the complexity of teaching a FL:

> Factors such as the nature of the subject matter, the interaction patterns used in providing instruction, difficulties in increasing one's

subject-matter knowledge, and the limited number of colleagues in the same field (Hammadou and Bernhardt, 1987) make it unlikely that a year of field experience in one school [by itself] will suffice. (Wing, 1993, p. 160)

FL education programs have also been questioned by FL education majors who feel overwhelmed by the demands of the curriculum. Students complete coursework that is often equivalent to a double major with additional requirements including the Praxis One test for admission to the program, demonstration of computer competency, block courses (including EDUC 4400 "Foundations of School Learning, Motivation, and Assessment," or PSYC 4305 "Educational Psychology," EDTC 4001 "Technology in Education," SPED 4010 "Exceptional Students in the Regular Classroom," and SPAN/FREN/GERM 4611 "Teaching Second Languages in Grades K–12"), and a senior year experience, among others. Many students prefer, instead, to complete a BA in the target language they plan to teach and seek licensure later via less demanding routes such as lateral entry. Moreover, students feel discouraged to become K–12 FL teachers because of low salaries: the average starting salary is $25,735 for ten months of instruction (compared to $30,526 for a social worker, $34,103 for a dietician, $38,744 for a civil engineer, or $39,042 for a registered nurse) (Gonzáles, 1999). Finally, FL teacher candidates hesitate to continue in these programs because they are aware of the frequently hostile, unappealing working conditions that most K–12 schools offer including discipline problems, unfair workloads, and lack of administrative support (Long, 2000). In rural areas, such as eastern North Carolina, the lack of support for the study of FLs at the school level is more evident (Ruiz-Funes et al., forthcoming), which makes it harder for beginning FL teachers to remain in the profession.

These scenarios are leading us to a dramatic FL teacher shortage that threatens the future and stability of our vision to strive for a more culturally tolerant and globalized society. Without K–12 FL teachers, students will be under-prepared to meet the needs of college level FL courses.

FL education professionals must deal with these tensions to satisfy each of these participants. Yet, they cannot forget that the primary goal is to prepare prospective FL teachers to become successful educators in the challenging context that K–12 schooling offers today in this country and abroad.

With the American Council on the Teaching of Foreign Languages (ACTFL) Proficiency Guidelines, the ACTFL Program Guidelines for FL Teacher Education, the completion of Standards for FL Learning, the documents prepared by the language-specific professional organizations—the American Association of Teachers of French (AATF 1989), the

American Association of Teachers of German (AATG 1992), and the American Association of Teachers of Spanish and Portuguese (AATSP 1990)—and the various on-going visions for FL teacher education, the profession has grown and, most importantly, is offering a framework to organize the knowledge and experiences that would help educate future FL teachers. Research on second language acquisition (SLA) is unveiling the mystery of how the human brain processes input to acquire and learn a new language. Today, FL methodology courses provide students with a basis for SLA and foster them to reflect on the premises of proficiency-based, communicative language teaching. Further, students are encouraged to put into practice the theories learned through the implementation of mini lessons. However, an important piece is still missing and that is the voices—beliefs—of the already practicing teacher.

It is the purpose of this project to bring theory and practice (through the experience of expert FL teachers) closer together in order to facilitate the students' (interns) transition from the "FL Methods Course" to the "FL Classroom." The initial goal of this study is to improve the preparation of FL education students at East Carolina University (ECU) during their Senior Year Experience[1] when the collaboration between the FL methods' instructor and the clinical teachers[2] needs to be strengthened. This project was funded by the Schools' Partnership Grant and the BellSouth Foundation.[3]

NEW VOICES

Linking theory to practice has been one of the main concerns in most teacher education programs. At ECU, the implementation of the Senior Year Experience has provided valuable opportunities to reach this goal. In this program, during Senior I—a semester before the internship—students visit the schools once a week and work beforehand with their corresponding clinical teachers, thus gaining insight into how the theoretical issues discussed in the methods course take shape in the real FL classroom setting. Then, during Senior II, students do their internship which requires them to teach for one entire semester with a minimum of fifteen full-time consecutive days.

However, the desired theory-practice link is not yet highly developed. One of the main reasons for this weak connection is that the voices of the school FL teachers have not been adequately heard. Seldom do teachers have the chance to comment on a particular aspect of a theory presented in the methods course, nor do they have the opportunity to describe how and explain why they implement a given theory into their own teaching. Their own experiences, beliefs, and practices have not been adequately recorded. Therefore, the gap remains between the reality of the FL methods course as seen through the eyes of the university instructor and the reality of the FL school classroom and its teacher.

During the last two decades, the FL teaching profession has been challenged by a substantial growth of knowledge (Cook, 1996; Shrum and Glisan, 1994, 2000; VanPatten, 1996; Savignon, 1972; National Standards for FL Learning, 1996). This growth has, in turn, made theory even harder to connect to practice. FL methods textbooks and other resources offer prospective FL teachers a comprehensive view of the theoretical issues while attempting to highlight their practical implications. For example, some of the most valuable textbooks in the profession (Omaggio Hadley, 1993; Shrum and Glisan, 1994, 2000; VanPatten, 1984, 1986, 1990, 1995, 1996; Savignon, 1972, 1997) offer a link between theory and practice. They either provide sample activities, sample tests, and sample lesson plans or else they provide classroom scenarios which invite students to reflect on possible situations they may encounter later in their teaching experience. Both of these practices are excellent, yet more is needed.

In addition, a number of other pedagogical issues (not unique to FL teaching but that have proven to be of crucial significance in the preparation of FL teachers) are seldom treated in FL methods textbooks. Some of the most important issues are class participation, discipline, and motivation within the context of a FL classroom.

This book, therefore, aims at offering a realistic connection between theory and practice while making it clear and accessible to both prospective and beginning FL teachers. Through action research (see Chapter 2) I was able to capture the beliefs and experiences of successful practicing FL teachers and link their experiences with the theories that lead the profession. The rationale for the use of action research and the methodology of the study are presented in the following chapter.

2

Collaborating through Action Research

WHY ACTION RESEARCH?

S. N. Oja and G. J. Pine (1983), L. Street (1986), D. Goswami and P. R. Stillman (1987), and A. Lieberman (1986), among others, have provided ample evidence of the positive personal and professional effects that engaging in action research has on the practitioner. Through action research teachers acquire the knowledge and develop skills in research methods and applications that help them become more aware of the options and possibilities for change while they become more critical and reflective about their own practices: "teachers engaging in action research attend more carefully to their methods, their perception and understandings, and their whole approach to the teaching process" (ECU Research Symposium, 1998, p. 1). This type of research leads teachers to reevaluate current theories and challenges what is known about teaching, learning, and schooling.

Action research is important because, as has been said: "Teachers often leave a mark on their students, but they seldom leave a mark on their profession" (Wolfe, 1989), and "through action research teachers will do both" (ECU Research Symposium, 1998, p. 1). Teachers, thus, become active constructors of knowledge rather than passive consumers of it:

> When teachers become agents of inquiry, the locus of knowledge about teaching shifts from sources external to the classroom (e.g., researchers, textbook publishers, administrators) to sources of practical experience (i.e., teachers). This shift enhances the professional status of teaching because teachers, through this knowledge-

construction, actively help to shape the knowledge base of their own profession. (ECU Research Symposium, 1998, citing Miller and Pine, 1990, and Johnson, 1993)

Action research is important because, as John Elliot remarks: "It is concerned with the everyday practical problems experienced by teachers, rather than the theoretical problems defined by pure researchers within a discipline of knowledge" (Elliot, cited in Nixon, 1989). Action research is naturalistic, using participant-observation techniques of ethnographic research, it is generally collaborative, and includes features of case study methodology (Belanger, 1992).

A number of action research studies that explore issues in FL learning and teaching have proved to produce outcomes with important implications to the profession. F. Zéphir (2000) argues against a unidirectional model of FL learning that is influenced only by theories generated from researchers. Taking the experiences of developing practitioners as empirical data should strengthen and re-shape such theories. He argues, moreover, that "action-based research . . . is a viable option for obtaining both the qualitative information needed to make any kind of FL education model useful" (p. 19).

G. Crooks and P. M. Chandler (2001), in their article "Introducing Action Research into the Education of Postsecondary Foreign Language Teachers," emphasize the need for FL teachers to assess and reflect on their teaching practices using "on a small scale the processes behind successful classroom-based research . . . or conduct their own investigative projects" (Nerenz, 1993, pp. 190–191).

The project that initiated the work herein reported is a qualitative, action-research study based on in-depth interviews, journal entries, and classroom observations. This methodology is used because the project is descriptive and concerned with the processes of "how" and "why" of teaching practices (Hammadou, 1993). This paradigm relies on the understanding of cases in their natural environment in order to apply the results to its immediate local settings (University and schools in eastern North Carolina). Action research is: (1) *situational*: teaching FL in eastern NC; (2) *collaborative* between researchers and experienced practitioners: University FL methods professor worked together with four experienced FL high school teachers; (3) *participatory*: both the university professor and the school teachers engaged in the development of the research agenda; and (4) *self-evaluative*: based on continuing feedback of the results by the participants (Cohen and Manion, 1985).

The strength of action research is its collaborative efforts between teachers and researchers with the purpose to evaluate and improve teacher development (Lieberman, 1986; Oja and Pine, 1983; Tikunoff and Ward, 1983). In this study the researcher became a "participant observer" actively engaging in the discussion/interview sessions ensuring open input from the participating members (Hammadou, 1993).

GOAL AND RESEARCH QUESTIONS

The goal of this project was to bring a strong practical application to some of the most salient theoretical issues concerning FL pedagogy. The topics selected include: *the proficiency movement, input, the teaching of language in context, and class participation, motivation, and discipline.*[4] These aspects were chosen because they have proven to be one of the most challenging issues for beginning FL teachers and interns. Two research questions guided the study: (1) What are the beliefs of expert FL teachers in relation to: proficiency movement, input, the teaching of language in context, and motivation, class participation and discipline; and (2) How do these teachers implement their beliefs into their teaching?

COLLABORATIVE MEMBERS

Four experienced FL high school teachers from two school systems in eastern North Carolina and a university FL methods instructor were the collaborative members. The reasons for selecting these teachers were: (1) they provide excellent language models as well as pedagogical models; (2) they are concerned with issues of FL teaching and learning and are involved in enhancing their own professional preparation; (3) they demonstrate an understanding of an appreciation for a variety of cultures; (4) they exhibit high expectations with regard to students' potential for achievement; and (5) they utilize innovative instructional strategies.

DATA COLLECTION

Data were collected during fall semester 1998 and part of spring 1999. The following procedures and instruments were used to gather the information sought:

1. *Background Information Questionnaire*: The purpose of this questionnaire was to obtain data on the teachers' experience as FL educators and as clinical teachers. A copy of the questionnaire is included in Appendix A.

2. *Interview/Discussion Sessions*: The team met two or three times each month (September, October, November, December, and January). The university FL methods instructor led the interview/discussion sessions and videotaped each meeting.

3. *Journal*: The teachers wrote a journal entry at the end of each interview/discussion session to record their own reactions towards the development and the effectiveness of each meeting. The journals were collected at the end of the semester.

4. *Lessons Videotaped*: Three class periods per teacher were videotaped. These videotapes were used to analyze the relationship between the teachers' beliefs about FL teaching and their own practices. In addition, these videotaped lessons may be used to help FL interns study, explore, and observe a variety of effective FL teaching practices in authentic settings.

5. *Viewing and Discussion of Videotaped Lessons*: The videotaped lessons were viewed and discussed by the whole team. The purpose for this viewing as a group was to demonstrate the teachers' rationale for their own way of teaching.

DATA ANALYSIS

The data collected on videotapes (interviews) were transcribed into typed manuscripts for accurate retrieval and detailed analysis. These, together with data from the other instruments, were compiled into protocol sets. From these sets patterns were identified that document the teachers' beliefs and experiences in relation to the above mentioned FL theoretical issues.

The coding of patterns was tested for inter-coder reliability. Inter-coder reliability was determined by having the participating teachers independently code into categories a random sample of seventy unambiguous events identified. The teachers verified that the patterns identified did indeed reflect their beliefs in relation to each of the four theoretical aspects studied (the proficiency movement, the role of input, contextualized instruction, and class participation and motivation). The coding was compared to that of the researcher. The numerical percentage of agreement was 90 percent.

FINDINGS

In the following chapters the analysis is organized and presented as follows: *Theories*—a review of the literature of each of the theories chosen, and *Teachers' Beliefs*—a discussion of the beliefs and experiences of the participating teachers in relation to those theoretical issues. A significant number of excerpts from the interviews are included because it is the voices of the teachers that are important to this study. The participants' names have been omitted to protect their identity. The excerpts in Chapter 7 come from both the interviews and classroom observations.

BACKGROUND INFORMATION OF PARTICIPATING TEACHERS (BASED ON BACKGROUND INFORMATION QUESTIONNAIRE)

The four instructors hold a BA degree in Spanish or French and are certified teachers. They have taught at the high school level (levels I-IV, Standard, Honors, and AP) in public schools for more than eight years and have extensive experience serving as clinical teachers. In addition, they have been members of the steering committee of the East Carolina Foreign Language Educators' Collaborative (ECFLEC).[5]

The teachers emphasized the advantages of the new Senior Year Experience as a way to make the teaching experience a realistic one, to provide a more solid preparation for prospective teachers, and to enable interns to learn the process of education:

> It has proven to be good for the interns and for the clinical teachers and public schools. When we can *cooperatively* prepare students for the "real world" of teaching *and* keep them in education, then we know that the program is an effective one.

> It . . . enables the student interns to learn the *process* of education, which requires more time than the former 12 weeks of student teaching allowed. They are able to see more of a global picture of the school instead of a tunnel-version one in an isolated section of the academic year.

> [It is] one in which the intern can experience first-hand the opening of a school year, the week-long festivities of Homecoming, the planning for SACS, . . .

> The end result is that they will be much better prepared for that first year test by fire, which causes many to flee education.

Their experience as clinical teachers has been rich, varied, and challenging. In most instances, it has helped them reflect on the complexities involved in the teacher preparation process. In general, a successful experience as clinical teacher was associated with the quality of the intern including: being well prepared, mastery in the target language, and ability to connect to students. Furthermore, the teachers state that they have benefited from their contribution as clinical teachers as it has helped them gain new ideas from interns and increase their knowledge base. Some of the challenges of this experience for clinical teachers are: relinquishing their own classes and resisting helping the intern when the instructional process slows down.

The teachers listed the following as being the common weaknesses of interns: (1) lack of travel abroad experience; (2) inability to make the language/culture connection; (3) lack of confidence in their own language skills; and (4) difficulty in connecting to students.

> The weak student teachers were not confident in the language. They constantly made grammatical errors that even the students recognized. They lacked in cultural awareness of the country. They were unable to make the language/culture come alive for the students, making the latter lose interest.

> The intern was not familiar with effective communication with adolescent students. Material was not presented with effective repetition or stress. The intern was unable to exhibit a commanding presence in front of students who needed it.

The opposite was stressed as the strengths of good interns. Also, creativity, motivation, and high energy level were other assets of successful interns.

> These students were very confident in the use of the language. They maintained a good rapport with the students. They were "born" teachers, very poised, and very much in control. They were creative in their teaching approach and always kept their students motivated and challenged.

> They had very good command of the subject area.

> The intern had a very good knowledge of French grammar and syntax. She also came from a family that had spoken French at home in the past when living in Canada, thus there was good command of speaking skills. The intern had also spent a good amount of time in France which is critical for being a good language instructor.

> They have been well prepared in the language and most have traveled, which means they have some degree of cultural knowledge that cannot be gained in a classroom. They relate well to my students and have had good rapport with them. They seem to have a "teachable" spirit and are willing to learn and try new ideas.

Table 2.1
Demographic Information in Pitt County and Greenville

	Pitt County (including Greenville)	Greenville
All Persons	126,263	56,788
White	80,656	35,843
Black	41,052	18,850
American Indian, Eskimo, or Aleut	541	391
Asian or Pacific Islanders	1,171	837
Other race	2,843	867
Hispanic origin	3,501	1, 244
White (not of Hispanic origin)	79,823	35,418

Source: Chamber of Commerce, Greenville, NC.

ABOUT THE SCHOOLS AND THEIR SETTINGS

The northern area of eastern North Carolina is primarily a rural region. It attracts a significant number of migrant workers who work on the tobacco and cotton fields. The main city in this area is Greenville, located in Pitt County. Greenville has become the industrial hub of eastern North Carolina with major industries such as Catalyca, ASMO, Rubbermaid, NCCO, and HammockSource. Pitt County is a thriving area with a population growing faster than the North Carolina average. A special census study conducted from April 29 to June 13, 1998 indicated that the population in this region is diversifying. For example, the Hispanic population has increased from 0.9 percent in 1990 to 3 percent in 1998; the American Indian and Asian Pacific populations have increased by 0.2 percent. Table 2.1 shows additional demographic data from the census:

The University and the High Schools

Three educational institutions located in eastern North Carolina collaborated in this project: East Carolina University, J. H. Rose High School, and Washington High School. A description of the three settings follows.

East Carolina University

Originally a small state-supported teacher training school evolved first into a liberal arts college (1947); a state university (1967); a constituent institution of the University of North Carolina (1972); and finally a Doctoral/Research university-Intensive (1998), one that "typically offers a wide range of baccalaureate programs, and is committed to graduate education through the doctrate. It awards at least ten doctoral degrees per year across three or more disciplines, or at least 20 doctoral degrees per year overall" (Carnegie Classification of Institutions of Higher Education). East Carolina is the third largest university in North Carolina with an enrollment of nearly 18,000. Both East Carolina's teacher education and heath sciences programs have earned national reputation.

The High Schools

Both J. H. Rose High School and Washington High School provide a rich learning environment to students. The former is located in Greenville and is the urban school of the area. The latter is located in the heart of Washington, NC, a small city twenty minutes east of Greenville. The student population in both schools is quite similar and so is the curriculum. The main difference is the schedule. Rose High School operates under the regular schedule (five classes, each fifty-five minutes long), whereas the other uses block schedule (three classes, each ninety minutes long). The foreign language department of each school is well formed with highly qualified teachers and a solid curriculum. Teachers from both schools have actively participated with faculty members from East Carolina University in projects (such as the High School to College Articulation Project funded by the Modern Language Association) and collaborative meetings (such as the East Carolina Foreign Language Educators' Collaborative).

3

Proficiency Is the Organizing Principle

For more than a decade now, proficiency has been highly advocated by foreign language professionals at all levels as the organizing principle around which to design instruction.[6] The word proficiency has been used for years as equivalent to good, fluent, and competent, yet it is the ACTFL Proficiency Guidelines[7] that have helped provide an operational definition for this term and a construct to examine and assess the performance of FL learners:

> Proficiency is not defined as a series of discrete-point equidistant steps or as a system with broad leaps and underlying gaps. Rather, as a representation of communicative growth, the levels describe a hierarchical sequence of performance ranges. (Galloway, 1987, p. 27)

The proficiency-oriented approach has been adopted by most school systems across the nation. It is now understood what proficiency is and what proficiency-oriented instruction represents. Proficiency is the outcome of language learning, and proficiency-oriented instruction is not a method, it does not represent a fixed set of materials; it constitutes a basic principle upon which organization is based in FL classrooms in order to help students read, write, listen, and speak effectively in a target language as well as to learn about and understand the cultures of such language (James, 1985; Spada, 1986).

Also, being proficient in a second/foreign language (L2/FL) indicates being able to participate in different contexts and perform different functions using the target language with accuracy. The trisection context/

content, function, and accuracy has led to a rethinking of views of what language competence and performance mean. Textbooks have changed considerably to echo the principles of proficiency-oriented instruction. And teachers provide students with opportunities to communicate in the target language in a variety of contexts while performing a number of functions with a reasonable degree of accuracy. In proficiency-oriented instruction, these three components—context/content, function, and accuracy—based on meaningful interaction and creative language production, are equally important, and curricula as well as classroom activities must be based on various combinations of them:

> The recent movement toward communicative language teaching has been associated with a broader view of language that includes not just its grammatical aspects, but also the ability to use language appropriately in different contexts and the ability to organize one's thoughts through language. That is to say, the recent emphasis on communication in language teaching is expressed in attempts to develop students' socio linguistic and discourse competencies in addition to their grammatical competence. In short, the conception of what it means to be proficient in a language has expanded significantly. (Harley et al., 1990)

Proficiency-oriented approaches are essential because, as supporters believe, they "are likely to produce FL learning and teaching that will better serve educational needs now and at the beginning of the 21st century than did the older emphases on structure, translation, and literature" (Crooks and Chandler, 2001, p. 132, citing Lee and VanPatten, 1995, and Omaggio Hadley, 1993).

It is this orchestration of teaching practices that poses the major challenge to beginning L2 teachers and interns. They often feel overwhelmed and unfortunately many of them go back to the way they were taught the FL, which tends to be grammar oriented. By listening to real school teachers who believe in the Proficiency Movement and implement its principles to their daily instruction, new teachers may see its application as more feasible, less overwhelming, and much more effective.

TEACHERS' BELIEFS

The teachers emphasized the following aspects in relation to the Proficiency Movement: (1) the importance and need for language authenticity; (2) the importance and need for personalized language use; (3) the role of accuracy and error correction; and (4) the importance of lowering the affective filter.

Language Authenticity

The teachers believe that language authenticity is one of the most essential elements in FL teaching. They emphasized the idea of making language authentic in the classroom by using videos, poems, songs, movies, and so on, to help students weaken their tendency to think that "foreign languages are not real." Furthermore, the teachers stressed the fact that language and culture is one entity that cannot be separated. Consequently, they pointed out the importance for prospective FL teachers to study abroad in order to gain first-hand cultural experience that they can then share with their own students.

> Language authenticity has to be used in the classroom, not only grammar.

> Culture needs to be incorporated all the time. Interns need to live in the target culture to be able to bring it back to the classroom; otherwise it is not real.

> Interns need to be aware of the broad range of cultures within a given FL language . . . and need to make their own students aware as well.

> Let's make our own small talk in the classroom real . . . let's see how the French will say it.

Personalized Language Use

The teachers emphasized the need to make language personal in order to motivate the students, to help them remember the language better, and make it easier for the students to create with the language.

> Make language personal, in that way students will remember it better; use personalized questions . . .

> Get involved with the school life, with what happens to the students in school . . . If you know your students, the personalizing comes easier, you have to dig down, have to ask them questions, become part of the school, get involved . . . students realize that you care.

> Discover what a student likes and then go back to that student.

Role of Accuracy and Error Correction

The teachers strongly believe in the importance of combining accuracy with communication and language creation. They pointed out, in addition, that students should always be encouraged to communicate in the target language without embarrassing them if they make a mistake. They all were in favor of indirect ways of correcting errors. Further, they stressed the need for FL teachers to use the target language in class as a preventive measure to avoid students' mistakes.

> The more they hear you using it [the target language] correctly, the more correctly they will use it . . . they will get the feeling of how it [the target language] sounds right . . .

> If they are creating with the language, I try not to correct too much because that prevents communication, creativity . . .

> You shouldn't expect them to get it right and use it flawlessly . . .

> If you want students to communicate among themselves, then it is ok to make mistakes . . .

Lowering the Affective Filter

The teachers believe in the importance of making students feel at ease while maintaining a good disciplined environment. This can be achieved, they believe, by being attentive to the students' academic needs and showing a genuine interest in their success.

> I throw my whole self into teaching. I am all over the room. I try to involve as many students as possible. I become a different persona when I am in front of my classes. You have to excite them, motivate them making students feel at ease.

SUMMARY OF RESULTS: PROFICIENCY MOVEMENT

- **Importance and need for language authenticity**
    - Essential element in FL teaching (to weaken students' belief that "FLs are not real")
    - Use videos, poems, songs, movies
    - Interns need to live abroad
    - Language and culture: one entity, cannot be separated

- **Importance and need for personalized language use**
  - To motivate students
  - For students to remember language
  - For students to create language
- **Role of accuracy and error correction**
  - Combination of accuracy with communication and language creation
  - Favor indirect ways to correct mistakes
  - Use of the target language as a preventive measure
- **Lowering the affective filter**
  - Make students feel at ease/maintain a good disciplined environment
  - Be attentive to students' academic needs

4

Why Use the Target Language in Class?

The role of input in the learning-acquisition process has been emphasized by numerous researchers (Ervin-Tripp, 1974; Krashen 1985, 1987; Gass, 1988; Heilenman and Kaplan, 1985; Lee, 1987; Lightbown, 1985; LoCoco, 1987; Long, 1991; McLaughlin, 1990; Schmidt, 1990; VanPatten, 1996; and White, 1989). N. Chomsky's (1965) language acquisition device (LAD), S. Krashen's (1985) input hypothesis, B. VanPatten and T. Cadierno (1993) and B. VanPatten's (1996) input processing, and T. D. Terrell's (1982) natural approach are some of the major theories and/or approaches that have shown that L2 students learn and acquire an L2 quickly and successfully when exposed to meaningful input. VanPatten (1996, p. 5) cites researchers who have contributed considerably to our understanding of the role on input in L2 learning and acquisition:

> The input hypothesis claims that humans acquire language in only one way—by understanding messages, or by receiving "comprehensible input." (Krashen, 1985, p. 2)

> All cases of successful first and second language acquisition are characterized by the availability of comprehensible input. (Larsen-Freeman and Long, 1991, p. 142)

> It is self-evident that L2 acquisition can only take place when the learner has access to input in the L2. This input may come in written or spoken form. In the case of spoken input, it may occur in the context of interaction (i.e., the learner's attempts to converse with a native speaker, a teacher, or another learner) or in the con-

text of non-reciprocal discourse (for example, listening to the radio or watching a film). (Ellis, 1994, p. 26)

For the knowledge system of a particular language to grow, the acquirer must have exposure to instances or exemplars of that particular language. Without such exposure language development will not take place. (Schwartz, 1993, p. 148)

These theories have called for teachers to expose students to the target language in all manners possible, orally and in writing (using the language in class, videos and audio tapes, texts from magazines and literary selections, etc.): "The purpose of language teaching in a sense is to provide optimal samples of language for the learner to profit from—the best 'input' to the process of language learning" (Cook, 1996, p. 129).

V. Cook (1996) summarizes the importance of input in the L2 classroom: it provides genuine examples of language use, it sets the appropriate tone for the class, it allows for genuine communicative interaction as input comes from various sources—the teacher, the students, the textbook—and it affects the "patterns of interaction between teacher and class and between students in the class, down to the actual gestures used" (130).

Two main features characterize input that is useful to L2 learners (Lee and VanPatten, 1995). First, it has to be meaning-bearing: "It must contain some message to which the learner is supposed to attend" (p. 38), and second, it has to be comprehensible: "The learner must be able to understand most of what the speaker (or writer) is saying if acquisition is to happen" (p. 38). In addition, input that is useful to L2 learners, particularly at the beginning levels, should be simplified input. This kind of input is shorter, less complicated, and produced at a slower pace than input used among native speakers. Research on simplified input has been summarized as follows:

Input to [non-native speakers] is shorter and less complicated and is produced at a slower rate than speech between adult [native speakers]. This input tends to be more regular, canonical word order is adhered to, and there is a high proportion of unmarked patterns. There are fewer false starts and there is less repair. High frequency vocabulary is used. . . . There is a limited use of pronouns. . . . There are more questions. Question tags and alternative questions occur more frequently. There is less pre-verb modifications, presumably so new information can be highlighted at the end of the utterance, where it is more salient. The input is higher pitched, it shows more intonation variation in pitch, and it is louder

Table 4.1
Characteristics of Simplified Input to Second Language Learners

General Characteristics	Examples
Slower rate	1. Fewer reduced vowels and fewer contractions.
	2. Longer pauses.
	3. Extra stress on nouns; half-beat pauses following topic noun.
Vocabulary	1. High-frequency vocabulary, less slang, fewer idioms.
	2. Fewer pronoun forms of all kinds; high use of names for "one," "they," "we."
	3. Definitions are marked (e.g., "This is an X"; "It's a kind of X").
	4. Lexical information in definitions that provide extra information related to derivational morphology (e.g., "a cathedral usually means a church that has very high ceilings").
	5. Use of gestures and/or pictures (drawings).
Syntax	1. Simple propositional syntax, short sentences.
	2. Repetition and restatement.
	3. Less pre-verb modification; more modification after the verb.
	4. Expansion of learner's utterances.
Discourse	1. Speaker gives the learner a choice of responses within a posed question (e.g., "Where did you go? Did you go to the beach or to the mountains?").
	2. Speaker uses tag questions (e.g., "What did he want? A book?").
	3. Speaker offers correction (e.g., "You mean he left").
Speech setting	1. Repetition of scenarios (e.g., daily encounters in a particular place).

Source: Adapted from Lee and VanPatten (1995).

in volume. It contains fewer reduced vowels and fewer contractions. (Larsen-Freeman, 1985, p. 436)

A more comprehensible list of features of simplified L2 input has been compiled by Hatch, 1983 (see Table 4.1).

One of the most basic ways to provide students with the necessary input is to use and conduct the class in the target language. This poses one of the major challenges to interns. Their main fear is that the students will not be able to understand them if they only use the L2. Consequently, interns tend to use their native language too often, translate or use partial translations in their lessons, or overload students with input that is not simplified or comprehensible. These practices create an ineffective learning environment that leads to the frustration of both students and teachers. Learning how real teachers in a real FL classroom use input provides FL interns with models of effective teaching practices.

TEACHERS' BELIEFS

The teachers emphasized six points: (1) the importance of input; (2) comprehensible input; (3) meaningful input; (4) use of native language versus target language; (5) proficiency level of intern; and (6) intake—language production, interaction.

Importance of Input

The teachers agreed that input is needed:

- constantly:

  You just have got to use the language constantly in class and . . . certainly give it a try in Spanish or in French. And, you'll be surprised. I mean, they really do understand a lot more than you think they will . . .

- for language production:

  . . . but you have just got to use the language in class. Or the students are never going to use it. . . . They're not going to ever learn to use the language themselves. . . . If they're not receiving that comprehensible input then they're of course not going to be able to produce language.

  If you don't use it, if you don't model [it] that and require that they speak to you in the target language all the time . . . then they're not going to.

- for language acquisition and thus to make the language-comprehension production processes natural:

  And you just keep doing it day after day after day after day and it does get into that subconscious, so they don't have to think about it.

  And, the more you use it and before long . . . I've seen my students [using] the French word "avec," which means "with." Some students have commented to me that they've been writing in English before and they'll suddenly write the word "avec" instead of the English word "with." And it's because you've just done it so many times. And I would say that the goal behind using the language in class is to get to the point where for instance: If we were having a class now and you and I sat down and said, "OK. Sandra, Sylvia, and Bill, turn to page thirty-nine . . ." We wouldn't even think about [it]. . . . The goal is to be able to say that in the target language. And maybe, they didn't even realize you gave it to them in the target language.

• to make the use of the language in class real:

It has to be real. You have to make your classrooms just as real because as I mentioned last time, they are still not sure that this language will work—that it is a real thing. They're really not quite sure at the beginning. "Can I take these words when I go to France and use them . . ." So you have to . . . use really good . . . situations to make it more real.

I think the only way you're going to develop a real world connection is if you're using it in the real world. And show them that this is not just a code, this is not just something that somebody invented and it's not based on English. It can exist in and of itself as a means of communication.

Comprehensible Input

They believe that the input provided should be based on material the students know (75 percent) plus new material (25 percent).

Seventy-five percent of your conversation should be things they already know. And then, this twenty-five percent is . . . just keeps moving along everyday because you keep piling new stuff in that zone. And you link it—the seventy-five percent. Like everything you're saying is stuff of the lesson. And you say, "OK, this is French that I know they understand. And then, once you make them comfortable in that they're understanding, then you start giving them the new . . . They understand that new [material] because it's linked to what they already know.

That twenty-five percent, like you said, will become useful only just based on what they already know. Because if it's just too much beyond their heads, it's just going to be useless.

Furthermore, the teachers described techniques to make input comprehensible, including the use of visuals and gestures, providing points of reference, and using simple sentences and repetition:

• Using points of reference:

You can make reference to . . . if you're talking about a dog, for example, they know that the dog has four feet and that the dog needs to be fed, the dog needs to walk and so forth. And so, if you're talking about a dog, they have some point of reference and so they're going to be anticipating some of that language anyway. And they can . . . pick up on some things just by knowing a little about [them] . . .

- Using simple sentences:

You do simplify and then, when you're still speaking French to them, you're using the vocabulary of the lesson. So, they know all this vocabulary and then you'll stick something in there that they'll know. You'll hear them. You'll see them. They'll know that you said something that they don't understand—that they haven't been taught yet. And then you say, "Oh, that's OK. We'll just go on and . . ." You have to slow it down and you simplify it and make sure it's a subject, verb, very simple object.

We need to be thinking about how children learn their own language— and how we don't give them big, long, complicated sentences when they're little.

- Using repetitions:

We say things in phrases and we demonstrate things and we repeat things.

The more you repeat it, the more you repeat, the more you repeat . . . if they don't know the first day that "Abran sus libros" means "Open your books," then the second day they'll probably know. And if they don't know the second day, they'll probably know it the third day. You know, everyone's doing whatever the teacher said. I think instructions—when you're telling the students what to do—should definitely be in the target language. Some of the kids will pick up very quickly and then some will not. They'll . . . follow. They'll . . . look around and see what everybody else is doing.

Meaningful Input

The teachers emphasized the need for input that is:

- applicable to the students' lives:

More applicable to their daily life. When you teach reflexive verbs, when that concept of reflexive verb that we don't really have in English. . . . You're going to use "What did you do this morning before you came to school?" "Well, I got up. I really didn't want to, but I got up and I went to the bathroom and I washed my face and I brushed my teeth and . . ." And then, what I usually tell them with reflexive verbs, "Now, tonight, when you do all these things, tell yourself what you're doing. Make it applicable so its . . . vocabulary you use every single day." You know, and it has to apply. It can't be meaningless.

And then, they're talking about things that matter to them. They're not going to remember it if it doesn't matter to them or if it has no application to their lives or to anything that affects them. You have to use those things that have meaning to them.

I would say, you're going to have to ask yourself, "Is what I'm teaching them today something that they can actually go out of here from this classroom and would actually, possibly encounter the need to actually say this today" . . .

So flood them with vocabulary you know they can use and that they will use and tell them to use it.

- interesting to students:

They would be interested in your family. You know, if I come in and say, "Well, my daughter graduated from Carolina and then I have another daughter who attends NC State." And some of them are going to be attending universities soon, so they're interested in that automatically—whereas if I just pick up a picture and show them a family, and say they have two older daughters and they go to x university, they don't care about that. But they, or if I know about some of their families and I talk about their own family and say, you know, "Well, he has two brothers and I taught his older brother and I know his older brother. His brother's name is John, and I taught him several years ago. And he's now at Wilmington studying. . . ." Then they're interested in that because they're people that they know or people that they connect with.

I like to get them to talk about five minutes at the beginning of every class just about whatever may be going on. This week we've talked about Homecoming because that's what's going on in our school this week. When they come in on Monday, I'm going to ask them what they did on the weekend. And I'm going to expect them to be able to tell me the activities that they attended and the things that they did. And they want to talk about what they did. So they're going to want to raise their hands and tell me and the rest of the class what they did on the weekend. And that makes it . . . more fun. Or, if we come in on a Monday and everybody's tired and "blah," I ask them how they feel. "Well, why are you tired?" "What is it that you've done that's made you tired?" And then they can really get into talking about that. Or they went to a movie. "Well, what movie did you see?" And then we can talk about those movies. And they get interested in talking about that because it is things they are interested in.

Use of Native versus Target Languages

The teachers believe that students tend to understand much more than we think they do; therefore, they recommend using the native language only when it is absolutely necessary:

> You use it when you absolutely have to . . . If you see they are really not understanding, then you say, "OK, well let's do it in English. . . ."

> But you should try, you should try and then do examples and if you see that . . . they're not getting it then go to your English. But you should try . . . even things that you think [they] might not like . . . like the subjunctive, you know. I do introduce the subjunctive in the target language usually. I may go back the second day and do it in English and just reinforce that. But I'll start with Spanish and illustrations and things on the board or things on an overhead and you can get those points across.

Proficiency Level of Intern

The teachers stressed the need for interns/beginning teachers to have excellent command of the target language and first-hand experience with its culture. This mastery will allow them to provide the students with the necessary input in class. Also, it will give interns the confidence they need to be creative with their lessons.

> I think that takes away from what we were talking about earlier— the realness of it, that the students may begin to question, "Is it real for you?" And it's funny how that seems to be a continual foundation of everything we've talked about in this group . . . if the intern does not know the language then, it's like we're building the house without the foundation.

> And in order to be really confident in the language, you really do need to be somewhere in that culture, some period of time—if it's only a month, if it's a couple of weeks. But you really, you really do need to travel.

Intake—Language Production, Interaction

The teachers emphasized the role of intake that results from input processing and the need for language production and interaction using pairs and group-work activities. They all agreed that input should not only come from the teacher but from other students as well.

> We do a lot of group work and so once they have the input part, then they have to take whatever it is, whatever concepts or whatever we're working on and work on that together in groups. And ... if that intake has not taken place at that point, then they would not be able to do that. So you're able to cruise around the room and check with the different groups and see what's going on. And they're pretty good about helping one another also. That's one nice thing about that group work, I think is that they're able to feed off one another. And if somebody has a weakness in an area then they'll help one another with that. And so, in that way, they're getting intake ... and sometimes they're getting input from one another as well as input from the teacher—which I think really increases their intake capabilities.

> Plus, they're really getting to practice and use what they're doing, so that intake that they've got is sealed. Once they use it, then it becomes a part of their language.

> I use situation cards and they don't know what's on the card, and I give them the card. It's in English. And there's a situation and then they have to tell me what they're going to do in French. And I'll use maybe four students at a time. And then, two or three days down the road, I'll use another four students and to see if they've really kept that intake, if it's really taken to their heads. And then, every once in a while, I'll go back and take out a situation card from three weeks ago and see if they've still retained it. And that's when you really know if they've really kept up with their vocabulary and their structure.

SUMMARY OF RESULTS: INPUT

- **Importance of input**
    - Constant
    - For language production
    - For language acquisition/language comprehension—production process natural
    - To make use of the language in class real

- **Comprehensible input**
  - Using points of reference
  - Using simple sentences
  - Using repetition
- **Meaningful input**
  - Applicable to students' lives
  - Interesting to students
- **Use of native versus target languages**
- **Proficiency level of intern**
- **Intake—Language production, interaction**

5

Making Language Learning Meaningful

Teaching language in context has been one of the major premises of the FL profession in the last two decades. Researchers (Walz, 1989; Omaggio Hadley, 1993; Savignon, 1997; Shrum and Glissan, 2000) have stressed the importance of context in the learning and acquisition process. Context is defined as the situation or theme within which students work with linguistic elements finding coherent and meaningful relationships. Context provides a framework that allows students to practice language in authentic, real-life scenarios.

Contextualizing the teaching of grammar and vocabulary has become an essential practice in the profession. However, not all approaches used respond to that call. The three most common approaches to the teaching of grammar are traditional, whole language, and input processing. In the traditional approach, students learn grammar rules and later practice using them in communication. This approach uses skill-building activities first (mechanical drills to focus students' attention on correct forms without requiring them to attend to the meaning itself). Then, once the forms have been mastered, skill-using activities are employed. In this phase, students use the learned structures in communicative activities designed to focus their attention on meaning and interaction. The main criticism of the traditional approach is its lack of contextualized practice during the skill-building phase and the disintegration of the language in small parts or sections. Comprehensible input is lacking and the teacher remains the authoritative figure without the participation and contribution of the students in the exploration of grammar rules and linguistic patterns.

An alternative to the traditional approach to teaching grammar is that of whole language. The whole language approach is top-down and is based on the premise that "language is language only when it is whole" and that it is the whole that gives meaning to its parts (Goodman, 1988). In terms of grammar instruction, words, phrases, or sentences are not linguistic islands; on the contrary, the linguistic elements only gain meaning when they are placed in context, and when used in conjunction with the whole (Shrum and Glissan, 1994). The whole language approach consists of the following steps. First, learners read a text containing numerous examples of the grammatical structure to be studied (Presentation). The learners work on comprehension, including identification of main ideas, details, purpose of the author, and so on (Presentation). Next, the teacher guides the learners to the target grammar aspects and together they work on patterns until they can formulate the rules of usage and formation of the new structure (Attention and Co-construct of an Explanation). Finally, the learners end the lesson with activities that require the use of the target grammatical aspect (Extension Activity).

Last, the input processing approach, proposed by B. VanPatten (1995, 1996), is based on the essential role that comprehensible input has in the development of second-language acquisition (SLA) (Krashen, 1987; Terrell, 1991; Ellis, 1990). Its main feature is its focus on input and comprehension processes rather than on the production processes emphasized in the traditional approach. In input processing the teacher intervenes at the students' conversion of input to intake (I):

> [It] attempts to alter the strategies and mechanisms used by language learners when processing input. . . . As learners process an incoming input string, it must be tagged and coded in particular ways. If the language is to be learned, the internal processor(s) must eventually attend to how the propositional content is encoded linguistically. (VanPatten and Sanz, 1995, pp. 170–71)

As in the teaching of grammar, there are a number of approaches to teaching vocabulary. They range from reading lists of words and requiring students to memorize their meaning, to engaging them in some kind of fill-in-the-blanks exercise, to semantic mapping and word association activities. However, it is important to remember that in learning L2 vocabulary, what matters is how the words are practiced. V. Cook (1996) remarks that successful learning comes from

> how well people remember something depends on how deeply they process it. Repeating words as strings of sounds is low-level processing and badly remembered; working out how words fit in the grammatical structure of the sentence is deeper and leads to

better memory; using the meanings of words together within the whole meaning of the sentence is the deepest level of processing and ensures the best memory. (p. 53)

For beginning teachers and interns both the integration of grammar and vocabulary and their contextualization creates a challenge. They find it difficult to link the teaching of vocabulary with grammar. This connection is important because "teachers cannot ignore that students have to learn not just the meaning and pronunciation of each word, but how to use it" (Cook, 1996, p. 56).

TEACHERS' BELIEFS

The integration of grammar and vocabulary using contextualized scenarios was emphasized by all members. The teachers explained the need to make the introduction of grammar and vocabulary authentic and meaningful to students. They stressed the use of oral work first in which the instructor is mainly the input provider and leader in the question-answer exchange.

I like to introduce at the one level vocabulary and grammar together. At the beginning, they don't know that they've learned grammar. I don't like to teach vocabulary in isolation. It's not very meaningful to me, and it's not very meaningful to them. We do the family tree, with a transparency—A lot of times I introduce new vocabulary on the overhead—but we talk about Monique or anybody in the classroom, and "Monique a un frère," she has a brother, and we learn the vocabulary and learn also the verb "to have" which is introduced in this chapter. We even introduce the plural of "have," "the grandparents have two children" so they know that the plural of "have" is "ont." They have no idea how to spell it, but they may have an inclination on how to spell it, they can say it, and we have repeated it. . . . I like to incorporate the grammar with the vocabulary—whatever grammar it is.

I agree that the best way is to incorporate it in whatever you're doing so you just don't sit there and explain it in English, "Oh, you drop this and you do this and you do this, here's a worksheet—go do it." . . . they've got to see it in action.

Grammar rules should be explained later, if needed, and students should be encouraged to discover and explore those rules on their own (either in class or at home).

No rules! No rules, we just talk about it. And then we go into the "you" and the "I" form. "Do you have a brother," ask your partner if he has a brother, and say, "No, I don't have a brother." So, we've included *avoir*—the verb "to have," and we've negated, and we ask a question, "Est-ce que tu as un frère?" And we do that for quite some time, with this particular lesson. So we've learned the members of the family, the verb "to have," negating it, asking questions, and there's a little preposition, another grammar point, when you negate, you don't say "I don't have a brother," you say, "I don't have *de frères*," and so, that's something that is important if you want to speak correctly.

They're asked to go home and learn them. It's in their book—and they learn it—and if they can't remember the pronunciation, "Well how did we say that in class, how did we say this with this overhead?" and they get the pronunciation pretty quickly. I think they better understand what they're doing—If they learn it at first, why learn the word for mother and father and not put it into a sentence that they can apply it? And use it with their partner, right away? You know, . . . even going back to our subjunctive, at level one they know how to say, "I've got to go to the bathroom," [which is] "Il faut que j'aille aux toilettes." So they know to use the subjunctive at the beginning, [even though] they don't know what it is!

You will have to get into grammar explanation—but when you can do it that way, it works. I think it works better.

The teachers favored the top-down approach although they agreed that it could be ineffective for some students. For this group, they recommend the use of a more traditional, bottom-up approach.

I will say that I have had some students for whom—they got to the point that that way is the only way they could learn, is when you really sat down with them, because they were just not getting it in class. And you had to break it down. You had to get beside them after school, and say, "All right, this is what you do now, you gotta drop that -er. . . ." And then you have to just sit there and explain it to them. But your first initial approach needs to be, perhaps, let them see it being used first, and then break down into the intricate details if needed, and a lot of times they'll pick up on the details (snaps fingers). They'll realize that in the -er verb when "tú" is the subject, they're going to add an "s" to the end of it without thinking about it. Just because they've seen it. And so, well, every time we've done that, it always has an "s" on the end and so then, sometimes before you even get to the explanation about conjugating -er verbs, they already know that it's going to have an "s."

The teachers believe that at some point in the lesson they need to check if the students are processing and understanding the rules appropriately. They recommend asking students to explain what they have just learned back to their classmates or any family member. Also, at this stage, explanations in English are allowed.

Sometimes I'll tell them, "You tell me now how to do it. You go up and explain it." I love to make students go up and teach.

Just to make sure now, in English, you explain to the class exactly this concept that we just learned, you explain to the class, to your classmate just to make sure that we all understand it. That helps.

The first night of every French I class I teach (this is the second year in a row I've done it), their first night's homework is they have a sheet of paper and it's a thing that they have to get their parents to sign it and they get a free daily grade of 100% if they bring it back the next day signed by their parents and it's a little thing that says, "My son or daughter, Johnny or Lucy, taught me everything he learned in class today, including" . . . signed by the parent (mimes writing). And I tell them, one of the best ways to study is to teach it to someone at home. Because if you can teach it, you truly know it. I learned more French than I ever thought I would.

SUMMARY OF RESULTS: MAKING LANGUAGE LEARNING MEANINGFUL

- **Integration of grammar and vocabulary**
  - Use contextualized scenarios
  - Make the introduction of grammar and vocabulary authentic and meaningful
- **Grammar rules should be explained later**
  - Favored top-down approach
  - Need to check students' processing and understanding of grammar rules

6

Motivation and Discipline in the Language Classroom

In today's society, school discipline problems are rising at an alarming rate. They are manifested in multiple ways from students answering back to the teacher, throwing away a test with a low grade in front of the entire class, to some very extreme situations such as raping a fellow student or using guns or other weapons. To teachers this is a threat that they live with daily. Yet, it is one of their most challenging endeavors as professionals to handle discipline problems effectively as well as to motivate students to learn. For FL educators this is no exception. These issues constitute one of the major fears for most FL interns and beginning teachers causing the attrition rate to escalate.

Seldom do FL students learn about class participation, motivation, and discipline in the FL methods course, nor do FL methods textbooks deal with these aspects. Instead, these issues are part of an education or psychology course where students review and analyze different theories, approaches, and techniques for classroom management, such as behaviorism, congnitivism, and humanism from a general point of view.

Considering the magnitude of these aspects, I include in this chapter a combination of theoretical and practical knowledge. Both the work of researchers and the experience of practicing FL teachers are brought together to provide FL interns with a comprehensive view of how to handle discipline situations and motivate students. By learning how experienced FL teachers handle these aspects, FL interns will be able to gain the practical knowledge needed to deal with their students with more confidence and a more solid preparation.

The theoretical portion is drawn from the research done by R. Gardner and W. E. Lambert, 1972; R. Gardner, 1985; and V. Cook, 1996. The practical knowledge is derived from the experience of the participating teachers.

Research suggests that there are some causes that lead to misbehavior that are beyond the teachers' control. These include students' lack of family structure, out of school violence, economic situation, and so on. However, there are other causes that lead to lack of discipline and motivation as well, such as student boredom, lack of challenge, feeling of powerlessness, and lack of rules and regulations. Teachers need to work on the latter and strive at developing a learning community based on rapport and respect.

Motivation, defined as the interest that something generates in the students (Cook, 1996), is probably the most important factor that has a direct effect on both students' class participation and discipline. Two types of motivation have been identified: *integrative* and *instrumental* (Gardner and Lambert, 1972; Gardner, 1985). *Integrative motivation* is learning the language in order to take part in the culture of its people (Cook, 1996, p. 96). This type of motivation reflects the desire of a student to identify with the target culture and people. *Instrumental motivation* is learning the language for a career goal or other practical reason such as a grade. Both types are important and one does not rule out the other; however, the former, integrative, may have a stronger impact on the student's performance in the classroom: "The more that a student admires the target culture—reads its literature, visits it on holidays, looks for opportunities to practice the language, and so on—the more successful the student will be in the L2 classroom" (Cook, 1996, p. 97).

A problem that most teachers face, according to Cook, is that the study of an L2 tends to be superfluous for many students. Learners tend not to see the need for and benefits of studying the FL. Furthermore, the students' motivation or lack of it depends largely on their attitude towards foreign cultures and their own cultural backgrounds. In this sense, the teacher may be powerless. Instead, teachers may have a stronger influence by projecting the right image to the students: "What they [students] think of the teacher, and what they think of the course heavily affect their success. This is what teachers can influence rather than the learners' more deep-seated motivation" (Cook, 1996, p. 99).

R. L. Curwin and A. N. Mendler (1988) provide recommendations for developing the foundation of a good discipline program. They stress, primarily, the notion that discipline involves dignity from the part of both the teacher and the students. Dignity can be achieved with mutual respect, good communication skills, and recognizing the limitations of students as well as those of the teachers.

Good discipline has been linked to motivation, which in turn has been defined with three facets: self-concept, achievement motivation, and locus of control. Specific strategies to increase student participation in class have been suggested, including, among others, asking low-risk, open-ended questions, monitoring the teachers' own behavior to see that low-ability students have an equal chance to respond, and exhibiting high expectations for the students.

R. Shockley and L. Sevier (1991) provide guidelines for maintaining control which in essence suggest that rules should be kept simple, brief, and focus on desired behavior: be prepared for class, respect your own and others' space, follow all safety procedures, be courteous to everyone, among others. In addition, they propose the establishment of consequences if the desired behavior is not rendered. These consequences must be applied consistently and fairly.

TEACHERS' BELIEFS

The beliefs of the participating teachers on class participation, motivation, and discipline were divided. Some believe in an extrinsic approach, whereas some preferred an intrinsic, affective one. For the former, extrinsic, the teachers thought that these issues were tied to some kind of external reward or punishment (usually a grade). They used an organized system in which students were graded on a daily basis. This approach was more threatening and had specific rules to follow. They associated "motivation" with "grade", "class participation" with "must speak in target language," and "discipline" with "cannot speak English." The last two were preventive measures.

I'm going to talk about my oral participation sheet, because I really think this covers all three of the areas that you're talking about: It's motivation, there's a grade tied to it; it also in a sense deals with discipline, they can't speak English without permission or they get an "F" on this sheet, and therefore in many ways that really helps with discipline; and of course it involves class participation. But basically . . . this sheet covers an entire semester . . . Each of the little blocks represents a day in the semester, so I have across the top, Monday through Friday. Here's the motivation and discipline, which is the rubric itself: They earn an "F" if they speak any English without permission or if they don't ever speak a word of Spanish during class. So, that's two reasons for getting an "F". They also get an "F" if they have not completed their homework, because if they have not completed homework, they really can't participate in what we're doing every day, so, it's motivating to do homework, because they're getting a grade here every day; and motivating to participate, because it's basically a participation, it's speaking and listening, it's oral and aural. And so what they have to do is they start with a "D" and can work up to an "A," it doesn't work the other way around.

In this system the teachers used a grading sheet and a rubric—a printed set of scoring guidelines (criteria) for evaluating work and giving feedback (both are included in Appendix C).

The intrinsic approach was based on the premise that students' desire to participate in class, to be motivated, and to behave appropriately should come from within themselves. The teacher's role then is to spur in the students a love for the language and for what they study. The teacher's success depends mainly on his/her own attitude towards the profession and the students. He/she has to reveal a genuine interest for the academic success of the students. The instructor's own motivation and enthusiasm will create the desired learning environment.

I think that participation, motivation and discipline are all intertwined as we've just said. I think it has something to do with attitude. If you are a beginning teacher come into a classroom with a great attitude toward your job, about what you do and the students feel that. And I think the participation and the want to participate not always for a grade come out naturally. They want to perform for you as you perform for them. I think as a first year teacher, you have to have that attitude. And again you have to project to them, "Yes, I'm going to learn to speak French, because my teacher loves, enjoys what she does and wants me to perform for her," and I think that in my classroom I have that projection, and all our activities, and all the exercises and everything all the group work—they do participate—I don't have to grade them every day as Sandra does. That works for her, I don't think it would work for me. . . . it's a self-motivation thing. And most of my students are self-motivated. They do raise their hands, and participate.

And you have to show them in some way that you're concerned about them. I tell my students, "I want you to succeed. This is not a place where I want you to fail, and get Fs. I want you to succeed," and if they get that feeling that you want them to do well, and that we as teacher[s] understand them, that we are only one of six that they have, and I think it just comes out, that you show it.

The teachers as a group agreed on certain principles that need to be followed in order to maintain a well-disciplined, highly motivated class:

• Respect students:

But respect them, and they'll respect you, and then you won't have any discipline problems.

Respect them and they will respect you. You're quiet when someone's talking and that shows them to do that.

- Have clear rules and expectations:

Establish your rules. Make them known in the classroom. Make sure you have these expectations and make sure the parents of your students know what you expect.

I tell them orally and write them down. And we have an open house at the beginning of the year where . . . parents come to see us. . . . So they know that there's going to be homework every night. They know what the textbook looks like. They know all of this. So, keep contact with parents. That will help let your principal know what you're handing out and what you expect and you won't have the discipline problems that you might have.

- Be well organized and prepared:

I believe that the attitude part is the big one. I came in to class and I'm all over the place and they just feed off of that. But if you come in the class and the first thing you say is in English and then two or three minutes goes by before you get your book out, and your lesson plans and your stuff, and you know, perfect chance to lose them. You're opening the door and inviting the problems. But if you're prepared, ready to go, you're not going to have any problems.

You model what you want them to do, and then they will do it. And you be disciplined yourself and they will be disciplined. And you're just setting that tone so much by the way you are. And if you start class when the bell rings, and you're prepared, and you have that class going until the bell rings . . .

If you don't have yourself together, and you're two or three minutes late getting class started, they have all this time to get involved with one another, and start talking, and so forth. That's when you have problems, is when you're not keeping them busy, and when you don't have yourself together, so, and that's hard as a first year teacher. It's very difficult. But if you can have your lesson plans structured in such a way that you have more than enough to do, so that you don't run out of stuff to do, and that you know what you are doing almost every minute of that class period, that you're on top of it and keep things moving, and it keeps them focused and then you really don't have problems.

- Keep students on task:

Keep them busy with work. Give them homework every night. Tell them you're going to check it. Maybe not grade it every day but that you're going to check it, and that it's work you have to do.

And you keep them busy the entire time. Kids get in trouble when they don't have something to do, when they're not occupied.

- Seek help:

First year teachers usually don't get any help from anybody. Seek the help. Demand the help, and hopefully you won't have that problem.

- Establish the correct image from the beginning:

You can't say it any other way. It's an establishment from day one. You can't get to October and then suddenly realize, "I should have done this. I'll start tomorrow."

The very first moment that they see you. That's when it has to happen.

You almost have to have a presence in the classroom. And because you are that way, the students are going to be motivated to be that way also, and you set an example yourself.

You will want to make friends with your students. Don't do it. Show them with your body language the first day that you may have a wall around you to start out with, that they won't get too close.

And that's true about having that wall . . . how friendly do you get? Because . . . they'll come up to you and ask questions and you know, and my personality is that I get friendly with students. It's just my nature. I'm involved in so many aspects of the school where I teach, from the football to the basketball game to junior class advisor—I've always got students coming to me asking me this and asking me that, and they know this about me, and they know that about me. And I've taken some with me to Europe and sometimes when you take them on a trip they see a different side of you, and so. I think you've got to— you almost have to be halfway crabby.

You have to be firm. But you don't have to raise your voice.

When you walk into your classroom as a first year teacher, you do need to, at the onset, and I think Sylvia said, make sure you set up these policies from day one, and that you go in there with a bang, ready to go, because since that was already done for you during your internship, when you go in, be ready to go, and have yourself ready to go, so you won't fall into that problem.

- Get involved with other school activities:

. . . one of the best ways for new teachers—is to get involved with other aspects of the school. Become visible, and the kids will gain a respect for you.

If you have a relationship with the students, if you see them some- where besides in the classroom. . . . They respect you, they know that you're a person, that you're human . . . I just think they accept things from you better.

- Get interested in what students do:

If they know you really care about them. That you take an interest in what they do—in their school life and their home life—and you don't go out of your way to do that, if you . . . just a couple of questions here and there will do it. And then they think, "Well, you know, they might really care about us," and then they'll perform for you and respect you and you won't have any problems.

I start my classes off every year (the French I classes) with a diagnostic test, just to see where they're at. There'll be an English sentence and I'll just say, "Underline the subject, circle the verb." Then I'll have questions like, "Tell me your favorite activity. Tell me everything I would have to know to begin that activity as a complete lay person," and they'll write and write, because it's the first day of school and they'll want to impress the teacher. And then I'll go and read them, and I'll put comments on as many tests as I can. I'll say, "I play the piano, too," or, "Did you see France won the World Cup this summer?" for all the soccer crowd—and they were writing, "My favorite sport is soccer," and . . . they get their papers back and you've written stuff on it and it's like . . . it's the most important thing ever written, and they're like reading what you had to say about it.

Any time you write comments on students' papers, I think it's just, you know, if they've been asked to write something personal, and they happen to include something. This year we were writing about families, and this girl happened to write about her mother being sick for an extended period of time, and so I wrote her a long note, and she came back to me later and said that it just really meant a lot to her. There was a student who lost her mother, and she wrote an essay, and I can't remember now, but she wrote something in her essay about her mother, and about the fact that her mother was no longer there, and I wrote her a note back, because I lost my mother when I was in high school also, and I explained that to her.

• Use preventive measures:

. . . preventive maintenance is a very good thing: I remember one day I was getting ready to give a quiz, and I had turned around and was looking across the room, and I saw a student writing answers on her desk as fast as she could. She was writing all the answers and it was as if I saw it and I just went (looks nonchalant), "OK Bill, watch [ya] going to do?" And so I turned around to the board, and I was writing something on the board pertaining to the quiz. And I said, "Guys, I'm going to do a desk check, just out of the blue, in about two minutes. And I'm going to keep my back turned, so you won't be accused, and if there's anything you think I could accuse you of, I want you to be sure you erase it." And I just stood there writing. And two minutes went by, and I go through and checked every desk and it had been erased. So we avoided the cheating by not ever letting it happen. And that's what I do about the bathroom across the hall from my room. I go in there, and they know I'm coming. Any time between the change of class and they know I may go right in that door and come right back out. That ends the smoking problem.

I will write them little notes. And there, that's another thing preventively you can do, like if you know you have a student who's emotional like that student I had. If she got a bad grade, I would write her a note and say, "So-and-so, I know you probably studied for this, come talk to me if you don't understand this," or whatever, and then you can avoid some of those problems . . .

SUMMARY OF RESULTS: CLASS PARTICIPATION, MOTIVATION, AND DISCIPLINE

- **Extrinsic Approach**
    - External reward/punishment (Use of preventive measures)
      Motivation = Grade
      Class participation = Must speak in the target language
      Discipline = Cannot speak in English
      Organized system: Class participation grade sheet and rubric
- **Intrinsic Approach**
    - Desire comes from the students
    - Teacher spurs love for language
    - Teacher's attitude towards profession and students
    - Teacher's motivation and enthusiasm
- **Certain Principles**
    - Respect students
    - Have clear rules and expectations
    - Be well-organized and prepared
    - Keep students on task
    - Seek help
    - Establish the correct image from the beginning
    - Get involved with other school activities
    - Get interested in what students do
    - Use preventive measures

7

Putting It into Practice

The following section contains a description of favorite activities, exercises, and games that the teachers and the researcher have used successfully in class. These activities can easily be adapted to any language as well as to any level.

TEACHING VOCABULARY

Personalize the teaching of vocabulary by asking students questions that relate to their daily activities/routine, likes, dislikes, and so on. An example follows:

To teach, for example, the weather, just start out by putting the overhead up, and talk about the weather last week. Even though it may be past tense, you're still getting the vocabulary in, or what it's like today, or what it's going to be like tomorrow and using pictures of what things you do when the weather is a certain way. Using the actual vocabulary page from the textbook will be boring. But this is so much better, to have this on overhead, to make it authentic, and ask students "What do you like to do when it rains?" "What's a good activity when it's snowing?" anything that you can do to involve them in it, and again, I love singing, and so for something like this, I'll teach them a song with the seasons, with the months of the year, or something. Days of the week, or, this particular unit has weather, seasons, days of the week, dates and all of that in it and so we'll also do songs because I feel like with a song, even though they act like they absolutely hate it, they really do like it. And they remember so much better. And if you go back and ask them something they've done in a song, it comes right back to them, because if they get the melody, they get the words back and so they will remember it so much better. But, you just have got to make it authentic—I was away for two days, so what I asked the students was, it was very foggy on Tuesday, so I just started out, just to get them talking, "What was the weather that day? Well, what happened Tuesday morning?" and this was something, this was a unit we've already done, but it got them to pull that back up to say, you know, what the weather was on Tuesday morning. I love teaching it. I make my students go on the Internet and pick a city in France, and they had to do a four-day forecast for that city, and they had to draw it just like the Channel 9 news, with the little (pantomimes lines) each day, high, low, and then the picture and I made them write the words.

DEVELOPING COMMUNICATION SKILLS

The following activity was suggested by one of the teachers who believes in bringing to the class "something" that is completely different from what they normally do, like a surprise activity that the students can expect to have every so often. The main purpose for an activity of this sort is to allow students to be creative and expand their communication skills. For example:

I will take from the newspaper, our Sunday newspaper, the "Hocus Focus" and you have to find the six differences in the bottom and the top picture and they have to tell me the six differences, and I time them, and they have to come up with all the vocabulary. They can ask their partner. I do that at the beginning of class. I might do that once a week or every two weeks. Just a little something different that . . . they like.

PRESENTATION OF VOCABULARY IN CONTEXT

To introduce family members and relationships, their professions and characteristics using "ser (to be)," draw a family tree of the teacher's family on the board or a transparency sheet and describe each member while pointing to the member and writing on the board key or new vocabulary words. The information is interesting to the students and some fun facts as well as cultural information are added to make this more appealing to the students: mi hermana y su marido tienen cinco hijos. ¡Son muy católicos! (students laugh).

Esta es mi familia. Mi padre se llama Hugo y mi madre se llama Tere. Ellos viven en Argentina, en Córdoba. Tienen un departamento. (This is my family. My father's name is Hugo and my mother's name is Tere. They live in Argentina, in Córdoba. They have an apartment.)

Vocabulary is reviewed and then students are asked to work in pairs and describe to each other their own family. The teacher writes on the board the type of information to share: name of family member and relationship, where they live, what they have in their house or apartment (review vocabulary previously taught), what their professions are, and what they are like. Students then share their descriptions of their families with the class. The teacher helps them add other relevant information (if the students hadn't included it in their description) by asking questions such as: ¿Cómo se llama tu hermano? ¿Dónde viven tus padres? (What is your brother's name? Where do your parents live?).

CONSTANTLY RECYCLE MATERIAL

It is important to review the material covered previously and incorporate it in all new tasks and activities. The recycling model—using and re-using in similar as well as in new situations while adding new material—is very effective. For example, students are taught greetings and basic questions such as ¿cómo estás? (how are you); ¿cómo te llamas? (what is your name?); ¿de dónde eres? (where are you from?) and they are asked to practice them in mini dialogues when they meet a new classmate. Later, students are taught how to conjugate "ar" verbs in Spanish in the present tense using them in basic yes-no questions. Students will practice this new tense with a partner asking each other questions such as ¿Bailas los fines de semana? (Do you dance on weekends?). Teachers should encourage students to combine the greetings and the basic biographical questions with the new set of questions. This should be modeled first by the teacher who would ask these questions orally to the students in class in the following manner:

T: (approaches student 1) Hola, buenos días. (Hello, good morning.)

S1: Buenos días (T and S1 shake hands). (Good morning.)

T: (approaches student 2) Hola, buenos días. (Hello, good morning.)

S2: Hola, buenos días (T and S2 shake hands). (Hello, good morning.)

T: (approaches student 3) Hola, buenos días. (Hello, good morning.)

S3: Hola, buenos días. (Hello, good morning.)

T: (continues with S3) ¿Cómo te llamas? (What's your name?)

S3: Me llamo Isabel, y ¿Usted? (My name is Isabel, and you?)

T: Me llamo Carolina. ¿De dónde eres? (My name is Carolina. Where are you from?)

S3: Soy de Maryland. (I'm from Maryland.)

T: ¿Visitas a tus padres con frecuencia? (Do you visit your parents frequently?)

S3: Sí, visito a mis padres los fines de semana. (Yes, I visit my parents on weekends.)

T: (approaches student 4) Hola, buenos días. (Hello, good morning.)

S4: Hola, Buenos días (Hello, good morning.)

T: (continues with S4) ¿Cómo te llamas? (What's your name?)

S4: Me llamo Melissa. (My name is Melissa.)

T: ¿Cómo estás Melissa? (How are you, Melissa?)

S4: Bien, gracias, y ¿Usted? (Fine, thanks, and you?)

T: Muy bien. ¿De dónde eres? (Fine, where are you from?)

S4: Soy de Virginia. (I'm from Virginia.)

T: ¿Llamas por teléfono a tu familia con frecuencia? (Do you call your family frequently?)

S4: No, llamo a mi madre a veces. (No, I call my mom sometimes.)

T: ¿Estudias los fines de semana en la biblioteca o en tu dormitorio? (Do you study on weekends in the library or in your dorm?)

S4: Estudio en mi casa con mis amigas. (I study at home with my friends.)

The teacher continues in this manner making the interaction longer as he/she approaches a new student. Beginning teachers should plan and rehearse this way of asking questions as he or she may not be able to improvise the questions due mainly to lack of experience. The questions should incorporate familiar material and target the new information. After this questioning segment, students would work with a partner asking each other questions of the same kind, beginning with the old and including the new. The multiple repetitions done communicatively help students memorize and acquire the material naturally.

SURVEYS/ENCUESTAS

This exercise helps students practice a target grammar point in an interactive, functional (questions and answers), communicative manner.

Students receive a piece of paper with the directions and the clues to use. A model is also included. The following is an example:

> You want to know what your classmates did over the weekend. Using the clues below ask yes/no questions to your classmates. When they answer "yes" write down their names and get additional information. You will share the information collected with the rest of the class. Follow the model.
>
> Model:
>
> Clue: ir al cine
>
> You ask: ¿Fuiste al cine el fin de semana pasado? (Did you go to the movies last week?)
>
> Your classmate: No, no fui al cine. (No, I didn't.)
>
> You continue with another classmate and ask: ¿Fuiste al cine el fin de semana pasado?
>
> Classmate 2: Sí, fui al cine. (Yes, I did.)
>
> You write down his/her name and ask her/him additional information such as: ¿Con quién fuiste? (Who did you go with?)
>
> Classmate 2: Fui con mis amigas. (I went with my friends.)
>
> You write down the additional information in the space provided. Then proceed in the same way with other classmates until you complete the chart or the time allotted is over.

Claves [Clues]	Nombre [Name]	Más Información [More Information]
Estudiar español [To study Spanish]		
Bailar [To dance]		
Ir a un concierto [To go to a concert]		
Almorzar en la cafetería [To have lunch in the cafeteria]		
Dormir mucho [To sleep a lot]		
Salir con amigos [To go out with friends]		
Andar por la playa [To walk on the beach]		
Hacer la tarea [To do homework]		
Conducir un auto [To drive a car]		

GAME: TENGO UN . . . , ELLA TIENE . . .

This is a simple memory game that helps students practice a target structural point such as verb tenses, numbers, or other vocabulary items. All students participate. The game starts with the first student in a row saying a sentence using the targeted structural item (a sample sentence can be "Anoche dormí tres horas," if the target structural item is the preterit). The next student has to repeat what the previous student said and create a new sentence. The third student repeats the sentences of the first and second students and then creates a new sentence. The chain continues in the same manner until all students have had the chance to say a sentence. This exercise, although not entirely communicative, provides students the opportunity to practice the language in an interesting and creative way. In addition, it stimulates short-term memory through repetition and rehearsal.

GUESSING THE WORD

This is another simple game, yet interesting and creative for students. It can be used at all levels of language teaching. It is mainly used to practice vocabulary. Students work in pairs. Each member receives a card with a list of words already studied (approximately five words). Each student describes the words to his/her partner using the target language until he/she guesses the word.

The following is an example to practice vocabulary in Spanish related to vacations:

CARD 1	CARD 2
El hotel	El pasaporte
La cabaña	El aeropuerto
El río	La posada
El avión	La pensión completa
La playa	El itinerario
CARD 3	**CARD 4**
El buceo	El traje de baño
El piloto	El crucero
La aduana	Los cheques de viajero
El barco	La agencia de viajes
La habitación	El guía

At the novice level, students can draw and/or act out the words.

IMPROVISATIONS

With a highly communicative, interactive teaching style, students should not have any problems improvising situations in front of the class. Students should be able to act out a given role without preparation. This can only be asked of the students and be a success if they are constantly engaged in a variety of functions. The situations are open and should allow the students to produce in the target language what they have already mastered and are learning.

Some examples for improvisations are:

• Imagine you are in a Spanish class and meet a new classmate. Greet each other and start a conversation.
• Imagine you are at a party and meet a new friend. Greet each other and start a conversation.
• You feel like going to the movies. Call a friend and invite him/her.
• Your friend invites you to go to the beach but you don't feel like going. Give him/her an excuse being polite.
• You are at a restaurant. Order food and something to drink.
• You are new in town and need directions to go to the bookstore. Ask someone for directions.
• You are on the phone with an old friend. Tell him/her about your last vacation. He/she will ask you questions.

STORY WITH PICTURES

For this activity the teacher needs to collect all sorts of pictures, especially those that have some humor and calls for creativity. The pictures should be randomly placed into envelopes (approximately six pictures per envelope). Students will be divided into groups of four or five and each will be assigned an envelope. They will be asked to create a story using all the pictures in their envelope. The students will be allowed to use dictionaries and any other reference material. Each group will present the story to the class.

This activity stimulates the students' imagination while using the target language in a functional way (mainly narration, description, comparison, inferring, guessing, and hypothesizing).

JIGSAW PUZZLE

This is a very interactive, multiskill activity that includes reading, listening, writing, speaking, and culture. It is both interpersonal and presentational. Using a story (literary selection or created by instructor), the teacher will divide its content into several sections (this will depend on the numbers of groups of students in the class). Each section should be similar in length and complexity, yet different regarding the information provided. The pieces together should result in the complete story. Students will be assigned to groups (preferably no more than four students per group) and each group will work on a particular section of the story in the following manner: They will read or listen to the assigned section and complete the chart given to them. One member (expert) from each group will be moved to a new group. The expert will answer questions from his/her new group members related to the section he/she originally had. Likewise, the other students will rotate to new groups to answer questions until they all complete the chart with the correct information. Students back in their original groups will be asked to recreate the story. One student per group will present the story to the class.

END OF QUARTER/SEMESTER/YEAR PROJECTS

A number of ideas that can be used as end of quarter/semester/year projects were suggested by the teachers. These activities target mainly the *Standards for Foreign Language Learning* and the goals and objectives of the *North Carolina Revised Second Language Standard Course of Study*.[8]

1. Writing a fairy tale.
2. Producing a video.
3. Interviewing a native speaker and writing a report.
4. Producing a presentation using Power Point.
5. Presenting a poster.
6. Doing community work and presenting a report.
7. Researching a topic and presenting a report.
8. Creating a portfolio.

8

A Dialogue Established: What Comes Next?

This chapter includes a reflection on the following issues: the value of the beliefs and practices of FL teachers as complements to theory, the need to offer prospective FL teachers a realist view of FL education in American schools, and the value of action research in strengthening the collaboration between university and school educators with the purpose to evaluate and improve teacher development. The chapter concludes with an analysis of the latest breakthroughs in FL education including the move towards communicative language teaching, the design and implementation of the *Standards for Foreign Language Learning: Preparing for the 21st Century* (National Standards in Foreign Language Education Project, 1996), the work on articulation, and the efforts towards voicing the knowledge of practicing FL teachers.

BELIEFS AND PRACTICES AS COMPLEMENT TO THEORY

The exploration of the teachers' beliefs and experiences on issues on second language learning, acquisition, and teaching has enlightened what the theories state, and moreover, it has helped complement such theories. In all occasions the teachers' beliefs and experiences have concurred with what researchers have proposed and suggested to be done in the classroom, yet the teachers' voices make such recommendations even more applicable as they are seen through the eyes of the practitioner.

In Chapter 1 (Proficiency) the teachers emphasized the need for authentic and meaningful language use in the classrooms. They insisted on making language relevant to the students' lives in order to make it real and purposeful to them.

In Chapter 2 (Input) the teachers pointed out the need for interns and beginning language teachers to study abroad and have mastery of the target language. They highlighted the value of providing students with comprehensible input and suggested ways to make such input comprehensible. These suggestions were very much in line with the recommendations done by other professionals in the field. Lastly, the teachers were tolerant with the use of English in the classroom provided that it is not overused or used unnecessarily.

In Chapter 3 (Context) the teachers emphasized again the need to make language interesting and meaningful to students if learning is to occur. They saw grammar and vocabulary as complementary to each other and suggested ways to teach both in contextualized scenarios.

In Chapter 4 (Motivation) the teachers' beliefs were divided in regards to what approach to use to motivate students. Some prefer an extrinsic approach, others an intrinsic one. Whether FL interns adopt an extrinsic or intrinsic approach to handle behavioral problems will largely depend upon their personality and yet-to-develop teaching style. Both approaches, opposite in nature, should serve as the basis for critical analysis and further investigation. However, they all agreed on certain principles that teachers should follow in order to both maintain a well-motivated class and prevent discipline problems.

The dialogue that has been established with these teachers and among themselves has been one of the most rewarding experiences to me as researcher and to the teachers themselves. As researcher, I was able to unveil the whys and hows of these teachers' practices: I was able to understand their own process of internalizing theory and adapt it to fit their own style and purpose in teaching while implementing it in effective ways to the benefit of students. Yet, more than that, I believe that this dialogue has provided a unique opportunity for these teachers to learn from themselves and from their colleagues. This dialogue has given these teachers an opportunity to reevaluate material they have read or studied, or heard of before and give it new meaning with the experience they gained throughout the years. They felt they were making their own theories as well, which is what we should ultimately strive for. Foreign language research provides us with theories and models that guide our teaching, yet it is our responsibility to decide how to use, adapt, and implement such knowledge in the classroom. We need to develop wise decision-making skills and be prepared to adjust our teaching to the needs and abilities of our students, thus attempting to make our own theory of how foreign language acquisition occurs:

> We as teachers need to be able to choose . . . among the multitude
> of options that are presented in the professional literature and to
> know why we think these choices are best. At the same time, all of
> us need to be willing to be open to new ideas that lead to profes-
> sional growth and positive change. (Omaggio Hadley, 1993)

Entries from the teachers' journals reveal their positive attitude towards this open forum on FL education. The discussions provided them
with the opportunity to both reflect on their own teaching practices and
gain new insight and ideas from their colleagues. Most importantly, the
teachers valued this research project as a means to strengthen communication between foreign language teachers.

> I have found these discussions very useful as a teacher because they
> have provided me with the opportunity to borrow a few ideas from
> fellow professionals. Discussing teaching methods also causes my
> own idea-generating mechanism to accelerate . . . these discussions
> have also challenged me to critique my own teaching methods.

> I believe this research project has proven the need for greater com-
> munication between foreign language teachers for we have all ben-
> efited from hearing various positions and philosophies on issues.

> I gained a lot from these sessions. I hope to use some of these ideas
> in my own classes.

> I think it is helpful to have these discussions with one another. We
> are learning new ideas and confirming old ones. It's also useful to
> be able to put correct terminology to some of the practices you've
> been doing and reinforcing for years.

> The discussion today prompted me to evaluate my own teaching
> of culture.

And last but not least, the teachers acknowledged the importance of
studies of this kind to enhance the preparation of our prospective teachers as they gain a more realistic perspective of FL teaching in today's
schools.

> I believe this is an exciting and very worthwhile project. For too
> many years, students teachers have studied education theories and
> then come to a public school where the practices don't seem to
> match these theories. This project strives to bring the two together

in a marriage that will benefit the student interns tremendously. They will be able to see how to apply these textbook theories to the everyday work in the classroom. (Journal entry)

I believe this project will truly help our future interns to be prepared for the real classroom. (Journal entry)

DIRECTIONS IN FL EDUCATION IN THE UNITED STATES

Compared to other countries, the United States has a weak language policy, and foreign language curricular guidelines and systematic outcome assessments are practically nonexistent. (Schulz, 1998)

This is an alarming fact against which presidential commissions, politicians, business leaders, and educators have been struggling for decades (*Strength Through Wisdom*, 1979; Simon, 1980). Particularly, FL educators have been on the lead to enhance and direct the status of FL education in American schools. Some of the latest breakthroughs in FL education include the move towards communicative language teaching, the implementation of the National Standards, the work on articulation, and the efforts towards attending to the needs of practicing FL teachers.

With the proficiency movement in the mid-1980s, foreign language instruction shifted from a focus on grammar and vocabulary to communication. Communicative language teaching embraces the idea that knowing a language or being proficient in a language means having the ability to communicate in that language in real-life situations. The concepts of function, context, content, accuracy, sociolinguistic and discourse rules gained new value, as did input, intake, interaction, and culturally authentic texts. Communicative language teaching made our profession an even more challenging one, yet enhanced each of its components.

As R. Schulz (1998, p. 8) states "the far-reaching influence of communicative language teaching" is seen in the design and efforts to implement the *Standards for Foreign Language Learning: Preparing for the 21st Century* (National Standards in Foreign Education Project, 1996). These standards are the result of the work undertaken by an eleven-member taskforce "representing a variety of languages, levels of instruction, program models, and geographic regions" (ACTFL, 2001). Two documents were released: first, in 1996 the *Standards for Foreign Language Learning: Preparing for the 21st Century* (National Standards in Foreign Education Project, 1996), and in 1999, the latest version, *Standards for Foreign Language Learning in the 21st Century*. These publications represent two of the most valuable documents that define the role of FL education in American schooling:

Language and communication are at the heart of the human experience. The United States must educate students who are lin-
guistically and culturally equipped to communicate successfully in
a pluralistic American society and abroad. This imperative envi-
sions a future in which ALL students will develop and maintain
proficiency in English and at least one other language, modern or
classical. Children who come from non-English backgrounds
should also have opportunities to develop further proficiencies in
their first language. (Statement of Philosophy, Standards 1999)

Both at the state and local levels, teachers, administrators, and curriculum developers are using these standards to improve their curriculum
and course of study. With the leading role and collaborative efforts provided by the ACTFL, FL educators are assisted in the implementation of
the standards nationwide.

Another national effort to enhance FL education in the United States
is the one on articulation. The Modern Language Association took the
leading role in collaboration with ACTFL and other language specific
associations. With grant money, state teams are working on defining
common goals and expected outcomes that would lead to well-
articulated, well-sequenced FL programs K–16 (kindergarden to college).

Some of the state and local efforts that have developed models and
procedures for articulation include Ohio's Collaborative Articulation and
Assessment Project, Arizona's Partnership Across Languages Project,
South Carolina's Articulation and Assessment Project, Wisconsin's Articulation and Assessment Project, and Minnesota's Articulation and Assessment Project. These teams have served in turn as mentors to other
state and local efforts such as the Eastern North Carolina Articulation
Project (Ruiz-Funes et al., forthcoming). In this particular project, a number of issues that had a negative effect on articulation efforts were identified. The most salient issue was the lack of support for the study of
foreign languages at the county school system administrative level. Ad-
vocacy work is underway to help remedy this problem.

And finally, the work conducted by taskforce groups on visions for
FL education revealed the urgent need for FL teacher recruitment, retention, and relevant research to reach classroom teachers including, in particular, classroom implications of research and theory and practice
considerations. ACTFL, in collaboration with language specific associations, is taking the lead in these directions through numerous open discussion meetings, workshops, and conferences.

APPENDIX A

Background Information Questionnaire—Foreign Language Teaching Education: Linking Theory to Practice

1. Name:

2. Degree:

3. Language you teach:

4. Number of years you have taught that Foreign Language:

           I II   III   IV
5. Level: Standard Honors AP

6. Explain your beliefs on the following issues as they relate to Foreign Language teaching:

   a. Proficiency movement:

   b. The role of input (use of the target language):

   c. Error-correction and feedback:

   d. Lesson planning:

   e. Testing/grading:

   f. Motivation/class participation:

   g. Discipline:

   h. Block schedule:

7. Describe your experience as a clinical teacher:

   a. Explain your beliefs about the Senior Year Experience:

   b. Describe interaction with methods instructor/university supervisor:

c. Describe problems/weaknesses of interns with whom you have worked:

d. Describe strengths of interns with whom you have worked:

APPENDIX B

Goals and Objectives from the Implementation Plan to Establish University-School Teacher Education Partnerships: East Carolina University Addressed by This Project

Goal 1: To strive for continuous improvement of the teacher education programs at the preservice level.

Goal 2: The redesign of senior year experiences: to include a realistic introduction to teaching and a strong theory/practice connection (Phase I); to examine the field experiences to ensure connection to a sound conceptual framework through (a) adopting a developmental model for field experiences and (b) integrating field experiences into all teaching methods courses (Phase II); to prepare beginning teachers to assimilate into the school culture through (a) orienting clinical instructors in each field experience to be reflective; (b) to model the best practices in their teaching; and (c) to offer a rationale for their instructional decisions (Phase III).

Class Participation Sheet and Rubric

The daily grade of **F** is earned if:

1. You do not speak a single word of Spanish during the class period OR
2. You speak even ONE word of English without the teacher's permission.

From this point on, you must earn the lesser grade before you can be eligible for the next grade. In other words, you may not give me an original sentence at the beginning of class and expect an "A," UNLESS you have voluntarily answered questions in class, cooperated with your group, and completed your homework.

The daily grade of **D** is earned if:

1. You understand the class discussion AND
2. You have COMPLETED your homework!!! (NOTE: if you have partially completed (more than 60%) of your homework, you may earn a "C," as long as you meet the other "C" requirements. Remember that homework is done AT HOME!
3. AND you have spoken Spanish sometime during the class period.

The daily grade of **C** is earned if:

1. You have met the above "D" requirements AND
2. You have cooperated, participated, and been a VITAL member of your group.

The daily grade of **B** is earned if:

1. You have met the above "C" and "D" requirements AND
2. You have VOLUNTARILY answered questions based on home-work or other oral class exercises AND you have been an AC-TIVE particpant in class (not just once). NOTE: No matter how many times you volunteer, you may NOT earn an A unless you meet the original sentence requirements!!!

The daily grade of **A** is earned if:

1. You have met the above "B," "C," and "D" requirements AND
2. You have spoken an ORIGINAL SENTENCE or Question to the teacher, one which expresses an appropriate, timely opinion or concern. In addition, this must be spoken DURING THE CLASS PERIOD!!! (not before the bell nor after the bell). Also, there will be a pad of post-it notes on the table in the middle of the room. If you're planning to give me an original sentence, grab a post-it note BEFORE the bell rings, and you must write your sentence or question on the note and put it inside your oral sheet for that day. Otherwise, you will NOT earn an "A."

NOTES:

1. ON SLEEPING: Please know that you earn an "F" if your head is on the desk or your eyes are closed.
2. ON BOOKS: If you come to class without your textbook or work-book, you will earn a "C" if you have completed your homework and an "F" if you haven't.
3. MISSING CLASS: If you miss class due to a school-related ac-tivity, it is true that you will not be earning points for that day; HOWEVER, at the end of the marking period, I will make an adjustment for that day. PLEASE DO NOT miss opportunities because of these points!!! If you have earned an "A," your grade will be adjusted to an "A."

LA FECHA	LUNES	MARTES	MIERCOLES	JUEVES	VIERNES	PUNTOS
17-21 Agosto						
24-28 Agosto						
31 Ag.-4 Sept.						
8-11 Sept.	Feriado					
14-18 Sept.						
21-25 Sept.						
28 Sept.-2 Oct.						
5-9 Oct.						
12-16 Oct.						
AUSENCIAS				PUNTOS TOTALES		
	PROMEDIO ORAL / PRIMERAS 9 SEMANAS					/
20-23 Oct.	Día de trabajo					
26-30 Oct.						
2-6 Nov.						
9-13 Nov.		Día para padres	Día de trabajo			
16-20 Nov.						
23-24 Nov.			Día de Acción de Gracias			
30 Nov.-4 Dic.						
7-11 Dic.						
14-18 Dic.						
4-8 Enero						
11-14 Enero		EXAMENES PARCIALES				
AUSENCIAS				PUNTOS TOTALES		
	PROMEDIO ORAL / 2as 9 SEMANAS					/
AUSENCIAS SEMESTRALES		PROMEDIO SEMESTRAL				

NOMBRE: ....

Source: Sandra Stinson, J. H. Rose High School, Greenville, NC.

APPENDIX D

Complete Transcription of Interviews with Participating Teachers

SESSION #1

Interviewer (I): OK, well today is Thursday, September the 24th, and it's our first formal meeting to discuss the different issues that we want to discuss—relating theory to practice in foreign language teaching. And, we have the four teachers: SS, BG, KM, and SB. Today we will talk about the Proficiency Movement. I would like to get from you your reactions, your beliefs about what you have read. (The teachers have read an article written by Alice Omaggio Hadley in which she describes the Proficiency Movement and explains the different hypotheses.) So, who wants to start? Your reactions, beliefs?

T1: I'll start. I think that a good concept that they use in this particular text is that language authenticity has to be used in the classroom in as many different ways as possible. You have to introduce them, not to just grammatical structures all the time. They have to see these grammatical structures on the video screen or in a poem or in a song, whether it's at the first level or it's at the more advanced level. Of course, you're going to gauge your language and your vocabulary to fit the level of the class, whether it's beginning or whether it's advanced. I think if you expose them to little bits of elementary literature or elementary poetry . . . I had even at the level one. They memorized little poems and they get used to that kind of structure.

I: How easy is it for you to present authentic material to the class? Using the textbook, . . . is the textbook you're using bringing up that kind of authentic material you want to use?

T1: They do, but something can come up in the classroom, that "Oh yeah, well the French do that" on the spot and I think the "c" and those five c-words, culture doesn't stand alone. You've got to incorporate and I want to throw in something to you interns out there, that you've got to live in that culture. I think you need to travel and live in that culture in order to bring it back to the classroom, because then it's dead to them— not if you haven't experienced it, it's not real.

T2: You can't acquire it from a textbook or reading research or a travel brochure.

I: That's right. That's right.

T1: I know some of my kids—and you'll find some of your kids—they don't think language is real. They're just learning odd words or . . .

T3: Or . . .

T1: Exactly. Exactly. So, you have to make it as real or as authentic as possible with videos and songs, and just make it even more fun.

I: That's good. Yeah, great. That's an interesting and important component. Good.

T4: And in Spanish it's particularly important, too, that they get a broad range of cultures because there are so many countries that speak Spanish. And that you're not just talking to them about Mexico, just talk to them about Spain but that they know about Argentina and that they know about Peru and they know about all the Spanish speaking countries— that you know, they get the culture. And traveling, as S. said, is really important and pulling that authenticity in. And this year we're doing *Las Mañanitas* for our birthday song. [I: That's nice, yeah.] We have just done *Feliz Cumpleaños* for a long time and I said, "We're going to make this more authentic, so we're going to do *Las Mañanitas* this year." And that's the very thing S. was talking about—making things authentic, so . . . this year every time someone has a birthday we're singing it. You've probably heard it a lot.

T1: I think we heard it in the last week or so.

T4: S. is right next door to me, so she hears the singing all the time.

I: So you can sing it . . .

T1: So it's easy to pick up language. It is written at the beginning but yet out of this memory, out of the song, "Oh yeah. So, that's how you say that." And they remember the song because they have it instilled in their brain, that vocabulary and come test time, if they don't know that word, "That song. It was in the song." And so they can pull from it.

I: More meaningful.

T1: It does make it more meaningful.

T4: Plus, I think that if you can, with whatever you're working on in class, whether it's grammar or culture, I think you can make it personal to them in some way. If you can get them to use it in a personal way, they're going to remember it so much better than if it's just in your textbook. What's a good example? If you're studying food, for example. We were talking today about eating out, and they had a reading in their text about a girl in Spain and what her family liked to do when they eat out. And then they had a guy in Mexico and what his family likes to when he eats out and so I just turned it back to them. I said, "OK, what do you like to do when you eat out? When you don't eat at home, what do you do? Where do you go? When do you go there and why do you go there? Why do you choose that particular place?" And then, you know, put them in groups and have them discuss it. And when you personalize it, then when they have it on a test, they remember doing that and it just makes it so much easier for them to create language when you make it personal.

T2: That relates so well to what I'm doing this year. I am working on TPRS, which is Total Physical Response Storytelling. You have a text-book. You work with words storytelling, you incorporate everything in the story. And you start with some key words. You might have "cat," "house," and "eats." And what you do is, you work with each word. And somehow, through a gesture or something. I'm using sign language to teach these words. So, we have "cat" and we have "house" and we have "eats." And so we learn and then what you do is, like you said, personalize it. "Do you have a cat?" "What's your cat's name?" "Does your cat live in your mouth?" "Does your cat stay on your head?" "Eat . . . do you eat hamburgers?" "Does your cat eat mice?" you know, and so on, and so on, and so forth. And, they remember these things. And then we build a story of, like a mini-situation, with all three words, like . . . "The big . . . student in our class has a cat who eats big rats in the house. How disgusting." You know, they think that's hysterical. But if you personalize it and you add more words, because eventually the story will have anywhere from twelve to fifteen words or phrases. But they just get a stitch out of making ridiculous situations. And the more ridiculous, the better they remember it.

T1: That's true. That's true.

T2: And that's been . . . I've noticed, they really, really do pay attention then, when it involves, you know, their classmates or the whole class. You know, we're "in bloom." We've done really crazy things. But everything is possible because it's taking place here.

T4: And doing that in all levels, or . . . ?

T2: Yes. I've attached to Level Two and Level Three this year. I don't have a Level One this semester but next semester I will . . . so which is where I really, really wanted to start it, but no, I just thought, "I'm going to go ahead." And I had gone to a workshop on this and they said, "Sure, go ahead. Just start, jump in and see what happens." And so far, so good. In my advanced levels, we've just finished a chapter on working in the future. But these are Level Three, so they had the "old method" as I say, the grammar, instruction, and textbook, and memorizing tenses and things like that. So, they already had a handle on it, so it's not so hard for them. So it'll be easier. It'll be interesting to see in three years what a Level One can do in a Level Three class. They're reading . . . I just got them to start reading *Goosebumps* in Spanish.

I: All right. It will be interesting to talk about the TPR when we get into other topics such as listening-comprehension because it emphasizes mainly listening than production. Right? And then, when we talk about input—important for you to use the target language in the classroom because you're using either Spanish or gestures but you're not using English.

T2: But I do use English. This method kind of "butts heads" with a lot of beliefs in that you shouldn't translate—if you go ahead and translate and get the meaning across. It simplifies things, why not? You know, it doesn't happen that often, but . . .

T1: They say that is not always all the target language. Sometimes you have to use English. If you're going to introduce, it doesn't matter what you're going to talk about, just to save time [Others: That's right.] you know. It's a complex structure that day. We're doing present participle. You want them to understand the concept first and then you give examples. And then you let them give you examples using the present participle in French. And then, you've got it out of the way, so I don't think we should feel that, "Oh, you know, not matter what . . ."

T3: I remember that you made a statement one time, not too long ago. You said . . . I reckon it just stuck in my mind. I remember you said, "English is their language." [T1: Right.] And there's got to be a basis somewhere. I mean . . .

T1: Yeah. Once you've established what you're trying to get across, then sure, you know. But . . .

T3: I remember something that contributes to what you said a few minutes ago. I have a statement in my class that I try to get across to the students, to make language real to them and that is: "Let's make even our small talk in French." Because what they're doing is, they're beginning to work on something and we've got them speaking and I'll say, "Let's talk about this. Let's use this now." And you call on someone and they're to provide you with something said in French. Well, they begin with . . . as they organize their thoughts, all their little, "Let's see . . . OK . . ." all that comes out in English. I said, "Stop. How would a French person say that?" I don't hear the "um." I want to hear the "*ah*." Let's make it real.

I: That's a great point, because that has to do with discourse strategies. And we sometimes don't have the time to teach that. We think that's not that important, but it is.

T3: You also have to be aware of who's sitting in your classroom. And I love to get involved in other aspects of the school such as sports and things, because then I can have an idea of who is sitting in the classroom. I have a student whose name is T. He's an excellent basketball player and he's in my French One this year and something the other day . . . I was writing on the board something and I made a mistake. And I caught myself. I said, "Oops, misspelled that" and I just erased it and rewrote it. And then I turned around and I said, "My fault, my fault." And then it hit me, "boom": There's a bunch of athletes in this room right now. "And guys, what's something you say when, if T. is driving down the court and he passes off and loses the ball?" And I said, "Let's say it in French." And so you've got to make it real. You got to make it come alive. It's got to come off the page and they've got to realize, this is not just a way to talk about whatever's here. [Others: Right.] "I can actually use this to communicate."

T2: They really don't want to read about. . . . [Others: Right.] It doesn't interest them that much.

T3: Right.

I: And what happens in your mind? Are you all the time thinking about, "How can I make it real or meaningful to them?" while you are teaching? Or does it just come naturally? Or are you all the time thinking purposely when you are teaching: "Oh, I have to find ways to make it real."

T1: That's when you have to use it all the time, you know. That's when you have to use it all the time. They have to ask the question. They have to try to acclimate themselves to say this or that instead of "there it is" to their friend. They have to concentrate on that. I worry all the time. My worries in the classroom are, "Do they understand?" You know, "Is it sinking in? Do they take it home and repeat it and repeat it until they literally turn blue and it kind of clicks after a while?" That's my constant worry. And I guess I'll never stop worrying that. My French Ones the other day said, "We didn't just turn blue. We turned purple." . . . I just worry constantly that I'm getting across and that they're using it . . .

T4: I think you do both of it. I think it just falls naturally [T1: Yeah.] depending on what you're doing. It just falls naturally. And then other things, as you're doing lesson plans and so forth, you know, you jot down notes as you're doing your plans. And you say, "This is how . . ." you know. And some things just follow that way. And they just happen and you say, "Oh yeah. We can talk about this now." And so, I think you have both.

I: That's a good point because I was going to ask you: "How can a new teacher develop that?"

T3: Don't wait for a teachable moment to come, but when they are, capitalize them because they are some of the best learning that you can do.

T2: Well, an intern would not really have a clue as to what a teachable moment is until a while, I don't think.

T1: No, they would not.

T2: So, you would almost have to create that situation, I think. And for a while it will almost sound false, you know, "This doesn't sound right." But I just think that is something that is going to come with experience. And all of a sudden you realize, "This is it, this is it."

I: Yeah, good. But at least the planning.

T2: Exactly.

T1: Yeah.

I: We have touched one aspect here, which is the authentic language use. Anything else on that topic? That's Corollary # Four. . . . Any other aspect that caught your attention or that you thought was interesting . . . ?

T4: Well, that Corollary One we just discussed also should the students just be encouraged to discuss their own meaning as early as possible after production skills have been introduced in the course of instruction. And so, as I was saying, after something is introduced then you turn it back to them. You personalize it.

I: Exactly. And personalize it. And make it more meaningful as well.

T1: And what B. said, too, I kind of wanted to put this in. . . . If you know your students. . . . The students we teach in the upper levels, we've had in One, Two, and Three, let's say. So, we've had them for three years. So we know what they do. We know who their parents are and we know how active they are in school. So, that's when it really comes, that personal comes a lot easier. Students that you don't know—they come in your classroom and you're cold. But, you have to dig and you have to listen out to the intercom to see what's going on in school. Don't close yourself out.

T2: Go to the activities. Go to the games.

T1: Don't close yourself out. Don't close yourself out to what's going on in your school. You become a part of that school and what's going on and get involved. And when the kids find out that you're involved, you have less discipline problems in your class.

T4: A lot less.

T1: Much less, and that really in itself I think is . . .

T2: Personal interest.

T1: It's so important.

I: That's great.

T1: But don't do it so much that you find yourself sleeping in the school and you don't have time, room for your family, you know.

T2: Our time is short enough.

T4: Even if you find out in the course of conversation, as you're talking with students that a particular student likes something in particular. Say you have a student that talks about the beach and going surfing all the time, you know. And then something comes up about that, you know, and then, you go right to that student and you have that student to contribute information and so forth. But that comes from knowing what they like and what they do on weekends and what they're involved in the schools.

T1: If they write journals in their class, you don't want to divulge what they're saying in their journal, but you can mention in class, "I know that 'so and so' (you know) likes to skateboard, or to surf." And you pick up things if you have students writing journals.

I: Wonderful. One of the things that is emphasized in the proficiency movement is these three aspects: context, function, and accuracy. Accuracy has to do with linguistic accuracy and discourse strategies. Functions is what you do with the language. You're going to be dealing with the past tense but for what reason? What are you going to be doing with it? It's not just conjugating the verb, filling in the blanks. You're going to be doing something with it. Describing, narrating, or you can use other grammar points to make comparisons or to make invitations—So those are functions of the language. And then the third aspect is context—situations . . . what I have seen, the student teachers—the interns, the most difficult part for them is to see functions—or to know how to do it when they teach. They tend to just teach the past tense because it's the past tense. How do you see that point? And that is hypothesis number two. That says opportunities are to be provided for the students to practice carrying out a range of functions or tasks, likely to be necessary in dealing with others in the target culture. How do you see that idea of functions, which is really an idea that was brought on by the Proficiency

Movement? Because before, it was just teaching grammar for the sake of grammar. So the Proficiency Movement says, "OK, we need that grammar, but for some reason. We're going to be doing something with it." How do you see that? What do you think about . . . functions?

T4: When you mention the past tense, which I happen to be working on right now in Spanish Two. . . . What I like to do with my students is to tell them as we start with "This is what you're going to use when you talk for example, about what happened yesterday? What happened last night? What happened in 1812? What happened in Spain?" And you know, put it in a time frame, so they can see that and so they can know why they are saying . . . that tense. And then what I try to do with them is to get them to tell me, "Well what did you do last week?" "What did you do last night?" Or "What did you do last Saturday?" And then you can also . . . bring in culture with that by saying what Picasso did with his painting. "He painted this in 'such and such a year.' " So you can bring in culture with that. So you have the personal . . . they know how to use it personally and then they also see how you can use it with culture. We talk about things that happened.

T1: Because at the Level Two, that's not the first tense in Level Two. You spend all of Level One with the present tense. So, they know that the only thing they can tell you is, "This is what I do in the present." "I do my homework." Or they can also say, "I'm going to do my homework." They can imply that future a little bit. But that concept—that's all they have. So, at the beginning of Level Two we're kind of tired of the present tense, yet it's the hardest tense of all. So we still have to review it every night—all those irregular verbs that we learned at the Level One. But then, like S. says, "Well, we don't know how to say 'Yesterday, I went to the ball game and we won. We don't know how to say that.' " So that's how you trigger it. I guess on a time scale, like you said. So, they can tell their friend, "What did you do last night?" "What did you all do last night?"

T3: I love the story-building process. [T1: I do too.] I remember, one of the things . . . I drew this from my mother, actually, because my mother is an Elementary Specialist and she's up in Virginia. But one of the things . . . I remember her talking about is building stories with students. . . . You're nothing more than the scribe and the occasional proctor of ideas and the occasional . . . "Well, let's correct that." But I remember the French book . . . the second level, chapter six dealing with the doctor— going to the emergency room. My French Three walked in this year and they could still tell me the story of a guy named Luke or Jean who . . . and they weren't in the story themselves . . . how he had slipped on the sidewalk around the corner from Notre Dame. And, he had broken his leg and the ambulance came and got him. They took him to the hospital.

The paramedics dropped him . . . as they pulled him out. And his friends screamed when they dropped him. Then the nurse took his blood pressure and they fixed his leg, and he goes home . . . and just the whole story . . . [T1 & T2: Yeah.] And in another story, he fell in a supermarket and all his friends laughed. So I had to pull up the verb . . . really quickly, and say it. "Well, we didn't have that verb in this chapter but they want it, so let's learn it."

T3: Because I've found a perfect way to use reciprocal action in French with the reflexive pronoun. And they . . . write it. I had no idea that this would even come up, but I didn't really stress it enough yet. I need to go back and do that. But, they wrote a story in French Three. We composed a story on the board and it was about a guy . . . our target was to use the current vocabulary that had been in the text. And so we pulled it out and they used it as much as they could in the story. And this guy goes camping and he puts up his tent and he lays out his sleeping bag. He goes to sleep. He's mad because he can't find a bathroom. And so, he has to wash in the river and then, after that he is awakened in the middle of the night by a sound. And he sees a bear and a snake. And then, the bear and the snake are talking to each other. That's what the students wanted to say. So we wrote it. The bear and the snake. . . . And then, using the reciprocal. And they just remembered it.

T2: They remember the extreme. One thing I was going to say, talking about how they remember the story. . . . Well, in the stories, that vocabulary builds up . . . I have student actors. They act it out. OK, and so if they fall, they fall on the floor. If they fly, they get in a plane and got to do this. Of course, I have to coach them. Some of them . . . So, I've learned who are the more reluctant ones, so you want your real "loud-mouths" or active ones to be your actors. Or you know, they go fishing—they've got to go fishing. And they love doing that. We've had a rat. We've had cats. We've had dogs. . . .

I: Okay, good. We have touched most of the hypotheses. Let's see . . . anything else we would like to say about hypothesis number three, that has to do with accuracy? So, you want to encourage communication, creative language, but also accuracy. How do you combine the two? How do you make sure that you give them all these opportunities to speak the language, to create with the language but at the same time be careful about the accuracy of grammar and vocabulary? How do you combine both?

T2: Carefully.

T1: Yeah, carefully. Sometimes it depends on the situation. If you just want the kids to communicate among themselves, then . . . you know, "If you make a mistake then it's OK, because your partner . . ." You know, we have partners in the room. "Your partner understands what you are saying, so it's ok to make a mistake. But always try to concentrate on that, the subject and the verb especially." You know, "Don't say . . ." [T2: Me llamo es . . .] . . . Yeah, and little things at this level . . . I'd say at Level Three, little things that you should never do. Level One, yes. But Level Two and Level Three and Level Four, that you should never do. So it depends. It depends and you do have to do it carefully. [T2: Yes.] You don't want to embarrass them and correct every word that they say, especially if it's a communicative exercise and not one stressing a grammar point. So I think it depends.

T2: What I do is when I tell a story, eventually they tell me the story and tell it to the class. First of all, they tell it to each other. And I don't pick on them too much because they're just working on it. When I tell it to the class, they respond something and say it wrong. And so you just work on that. I haven't said, "You're wrong. Stop, you stupid person." You know, but you just . . .

T1: You can't do that.

T2: You just have to be real . . . in the beginning, I think you have to be very subtle about it. Now, as you said, the higher you go, you have to go for more correction than you did at Levels One or Two.

T3: I think the more they hear you using it correctly [T2: Exactly. It has to sound right.] . . . I said, "Guys, if you're walking down the street in France, and . . . you walk up to some stranger . . . Well, first of all don't do that in France. But if you were to walk up to a stranger in France and ask them, 'Is the word *trashcan* masculine or feminine?' And then, that French person may or may not be able to tell you. But that French person will probably sit down and go ' . . . ' and then they'll say, 'Well, it's . . . ' And then they'll go because of the way it sounds." I said, "You've got to get to the point where you know that if I come in and say ' . . . ' then you're immediately going to go 'Oh, my spine just crawled. Something wasn't right there.' " And it's by sound. And that's why you've got to use it . . . [I: Use the target language.]

T2: So you go by what sounds right?

T3: Right.

I: How do you balance, again, linking communication with accuracy? How do you balance mechanical exercises, control exercises, and more creative exercises?

T4: Well, I'd like to start with the mechanical ones first, so that they get the concept of what you're working on and then move to the more creative ones where you know, they're actually creating language. And as we were saying about correcting it, if they're creating, I really try not to correct them much at all unless it's just something horrible. You know, because that stops communication, if they feel like you will be constantly correcting them, they'll hold back. . . .

T1: It stops creativity.

T4: And it stops creativity, you know.

T1: And it puts a damper on it.

T4: But, if you're working on a particular function [T1: Yeah.] and they keep missing that, obviously, you know, obviously you've got to say something about that. But if you're not working on adjectives and they don't make an adjective agree, then you know, let it slide, because you're not concentrating on that right then.

T1: But you shouldn't expect them, just because you spent four weeks on the imperfect. You shouldn't expect them to get it right and use it correctly, flawlessly every time. You can't expect that. And as a first year teacher, you're going to wonder, "Why aren't they getting it? Why are they all making mistakes?" [T2: "What am I doing wrong?"] "What am I doing wrong?" So, you know, you have to . . .

T2: Well that's the function of learning. . . . You have to practice it. I mean, it's just difficult.

T2: It's just like learning your own language. How long did it take us to become proficient?

I: Even you go to college to take some English courses.

T1: Yes.

T2: There are still some graduating who can't.

T1: It's got to be purposeful and meaningful. [I: Meaning, yeah.] Exactly. You don't just, you know, conjugate verbs down the hall. You know, "I am, you are, he is . . ."

T2: No. You don't do that. And, so it has to be meaningful all the time.

I: That's right. And that's the importance of this. It's not a methodology—the Proficiency Movement—but it is an approach to language teaching. So, that's when I tell my students, "We are in a beautiful time for language teaching, because it is so complex, and that language—it is now everything." You have to take into account all these aspects and this is a challenge. Because when the grammar-translation approach was alive in the '20s, it was probably too easy to teach. Just grammar drills, doing exercise and that's it. [T1: That's it.] But now it's much more. It's fascinating, but it's more challenging.

T4: But nobody was communicating.

I: Nobody could communicate.

T2: Right. They conjugated a verb but . . .

T4: They could conjugate verbs. . . . One thing that I like to do with, for example, making adjectives agree, which English speaking people constantly have trouble—they are forever forgetting to make their adjectives agree. It's just emphasized to them every time, "Every single time an adjective comes out of your mouth, or you write an adjective on a piece of paper, it's got to agree with something." So, if you know, "There's . . . OK . . . What does this agree with?" So if they say something in class, if a girl says, "*Estoy cansado hoy.*" And you know, I'll look at her and say, "*Cansado es un adjectivo.*" [I: Think.] Think. . . . an adjective has come out of her mouth. "What does it agree with?" "Oh, it agrees with me." You know, so then she can go back and say "*Estoy cansada.*" And, if you know, just little things like that you can give them that'll help trigger something in their mind and then try to bring that back to them, and then they can self-correct and that's even better because they'll remember [I: Exactly.] much better next time.

T3: I use a "chivalry approach."

T1: I say guys, "She is feminine, isn't she? And she's got to change that . . ."

T3: And I'll tell them, I'll say, "If you're going to be talking about . . . if you're going to be using the third person and you're talking about a woman, don't offend those French women."

T1: And as you put one and two and three and four years under your belt, you'll catch on and it'll be easier and . . .

I: It gets easier.

T2: You acquire it.

T1: You really do acquire it. But everyday is a challenge. [T2 & T4: It is. It is.] And you've got to want it that way. You don't want it to be the "same-old-same-old" everyday. [I: Boring.] And then the kids get bored. . . .

I: Good. Let's go to hypothesis number four, which probably applies to anything that you teach in your life—which is the affective filter, which is the student's feeling at ease with you—being relaxed in the class. [T1: That's part of personality.] Tell me what you think about it. Instructors should be responsive to the affective as well as the cognitive needs of the students.

T3: I throw my whole self into my teaching. I'm there from the "get go." From the minute that bell rings, I am all over the room. I'm involved. I try to involve as many students. I try to get to know as many students. I talk about things they enjoy. And try to let them see, "Hey, we can discuss that in French as well." And then I just say . . . I just try to be as . . . I don't know . . . I try to be—I can't express it. [I: That genuine interest that you have for them.] . . . Open. It's very hard to express. It just kind of comes naturally when you stand in . . . I would become a different person when I'm in the classroom and you sit, stand in front of twenty-seven people. It's just . . . All of a sudden, you just take a different mask.

T2: Persona. You are a different persona. Yeah, [T4: You are.] my daughter is in school there and I can't tell you how many times . . . she works with yearbook. She's walked into the room and my students say, "Do you know your mom is crazy? Do you know what she does in class?" you know. I mean, yeah, I jump up and down and fall and you know, you do. You've got to excite them and motivate them. And I tell them, "Look, if I can do this, you should be able to. Just feel free." And I try to encourage them that you know, they can do stuff with me and do things in class. Be crazy, silly, or whatever. It's OK. And then, they have a hard time. You know, you see them in the hall doing all this stuff and then they get in your classroom and they want to act like they don't know what they want to do. But if you can "let your hair down" so to speak with them . . . and I do. I'm like B. I'm just a different person than I am at home.

I: How do you balance making the students feel comfortable with you and at ease and discipline?

T2: Well, you have to have guidelines. . . . You really do have to have rules.

T3: I'm a believer in that if your lessons are well planned, and you know exactly what you have got planned for that day, and you've got everything organized, where you're not going to have to stop right in the middle of the lesson and say, "Oh brother, where did I put that stack of stuff I was going to give?" If everything and every single minute is planned out, that is half of your discipline problems [T4: It is.] there. . . . I believe in preventive maintenance.

T2: Even after you learn . . . I don't have any discipline problems, really. I had everything planned. . . . My main topic problem is, they're using these words and they want to talk to each other . . . "OK, wait. Later. '*Más tarde.*' " And that's because you, with this particular approach, you really have to expect a little bit more noise than you would . . . an orderly classroom is not, you know, I mean . . . I don't know. I'm not saying it right but they're enjoying themselves. It's just hard when I say, "OK, stop. Go on to the next one and see how you can use it." But you have the guidelines set up and then work within that. But I have not had any discipline problems so far.

T4: Language classrooms are so much more interactive than other subject areas are. And so you are going to have more noise level in a language classroom because you want them participating. [T2: Right.] Because you want them speaking. Not only to you but to one another so they're getting a lot more practice. So you want them in groups, in doing things with one another as well as with you. And so, you're going to have more noise level but it needs to be the control. It needs to be [T2: You have guidelines.] what they have—what they know their task is and they're going about their task. And, you don't give them too much lag time, so that they finish. And then they won't get into trouble, but you have timed it so that they know, you know, "I've got to get this done in this amount of time because we're moving on to something else."

T1: And I think [I: Take your time and do it . . .] if you have group activities . . . and you must have group activities. You must have partner activities. If you have group activities and they have the task, they do the task, kind of say, "OK, time out. We're through." Don't give them too much time. Give them maybe a minute or two less time than you planned. And then you can start with the conversation, asking them questions or whatever. But that too . . . you can do that easily.

I: Good, great. Any other thoughts about the Proficiency Movement in general? Or any other hypothesis or corollaries?

T1: Did we cover them all? I think we covered them all.

T3: I think the Proficiency Movement is good. I think it's a movement that can absorb elements of other movements too. [I: That's right.] And in reality it is almost a potpourri of everything put together.

T4: It really is.

T1: But it's a logical approach.

I: It's a logical approach, yeah. And it's not imposing the methodology on you. Just take into account "this, this and that, and that." And then, do it. But it's not telling you, it's not only the TPR approach or it's not this. So you can use lots of different approaches if you want, but you need to have into account. That's what I tell all my students. You need to have into account all this. These are the basic elements.

T1: And I think you need to feel a sense of confidence. You need to be confident in yourself and you need to be confident in the language. [I: Exactly.] Because if you . . . if you're not sure about yourself and the kids start asking you, well, you know . . . you have to be very confident in the use of the language.

I: Because your role is very active in using the language as well. [T1: Yes, yes.]

T4: And they will ask you things that you probably, maybe never thought of. So if you don't know the language yourself, you're not going to know how to answer those questions that they come up with. Because they'll think of all these other little exceptions to everything, you know, to ask you about.

T2: But you know, even in that situation . . . because there are a lot of things I don't know and I'll just tell them that. "You know, I just don't know and I'll look it up." "But aren't you supposed to know?" "I'm sorry but I'll bet you can go ask your English teacher if she doesn't know everything there is to know about it." You know, and so I think lots of times when you let them know that you are a human being—because sometimes they think of you as the strange person in the classroom, but you can admit to human error and things like that. Then say, "You know, let me just get back to you on that." And they say, "OK." And when you do, you go up just a little bit more.

T4: You have them look it up.

T2: Yeah, they can look it up.

T4: Have them look it up.

I: Good.

T3: And never stop learning the language. [T2: No.] If it's not your native language . . . I'm learning more French all the time.

T2: In Spanish, with twenty countries that speak it, variations of everything in every country . . . [T4: That's right.] you would never, you would never know it all.

T4: There's no way. There's no way.

I: Even a native speaker would not know. [T2: No.]

T4: You get a native speaker—and we have a lot of native speakers here . . . —in your class and the native speakers from Venezuela—and doesn't know the terminology that's used in Spain, you know. And you're working with something with that and they have no idea.

I: Exactly, yeah. Good point, great. All right . . .

SESSION #2

I: OK, today is October the 8th. This is our second meeting. We are going to talk about input.

T4: I thought that the article was very good. You know, basically it is saying that the students have got to have that comprehensible input . . . if they're not receiving that comprehensible input then they're of course not going to be able to produce language. And I really liked the examples that they gave of parents talking to children. And how in certainly the beginning level language class, those are the type of things that we need to be doing. We need to be thinking about how children learn their own language—and how we don't give them big, long, complicated sentences when they're little. We say things in phrases and we demonstrate things and we repeat things. And I thought it was also interesting the way they talked about not correcting what they're saying. I remember the example about the child who lost a truck under the chair and he said, "Truck fall, fall." And the mother didn't say, "No, that's wrong. Don't say it that way." She just repeated, "The truck fell down." [I: Just the correct form.] Just giving them the correct back, which in a language classroom is certainly something that you want to do—giving them correct language back and not always saying, you know, "That's the wrong way to say that." But, just when you hear things like that, just following up and reinforcing and confirming. So, I thought that was good.

I: Good, great.

T1: And I think that as a first year teacher . . . I know when I started out teaching, I wanted all of my students to speak correctly and not make any mistakes. And now I find myself, "As long as they're communicating and the rest of the class understands what they're saying—so big deal. They're communicating." No one's perfect, but then I tell them, "When you write it down" [T4: That's right.], that's when it becomes engraved in stone . . . the grammar has to be correct . . . if it's a test on the present tense, then we expect all the present tense verbs to be correct. [I: That's right.] So, I think that we should emphasize to our interns or to our first year teachers, that not to worry about grammar when they're speaking. [I: When the students are speaking.] When the students are speaking, yes. . . . What I do when a student is in a conversational setting—when it's done, I'll say all the good things that they've said. Then I might say, "Now, how would you go about say 'such and such' a thing?" And comparing it to what they've said, and maybe correct them in an indirect way. Don't say, "You can't say it that way. It has to be said this way." Just try to do it as indirectly as possible. I think that would work. And it gives the student more confidence because if you correct them every time, he's not going to want to open his mouth. And you know, they get . . . they feel intimidated. So, I think that's important.

T3: It's so easy to do that, though. It's so easy to get into that mold [T1: I know.] because the minute that you hear error . . . it's just like a natural [I: Reaction.] . . . It's some kind of "teacher germ" in you or something that just makes you immediately want to go, "Wait a minute."

T1: My students know I always pull my ear when they made [I: Make a mistake.] something that really, really sounded bad, you know, like "They is." I pull my ear and they know that it hurts my ear. So the sound just hurts my ear and so they kind of . . .

T4: That works for me.

I: OK, we are going to be talking about error correction in our next meeting session; I don't want to be getting into details of that but I do want to bring you back to input. I have seen that for many of the new teachers the most difficult, one of the most difficult things for them is to use the target language in the classroom. I think the reason is that they want to be understood by the students. And they feel that if they speak French or Spanish they will not be understood at all. So, what they do is, they overuse English in the classrooms. So I want you to give me your idea why you think using the language—using the target language is so important.

T1: The more you repeat it, the more you repeat, the more you repeat. . . . If they don't know the first day that ". . . " means "Open your books," then the second day they'll probably know. And if they don't know the second day, they'll probably know it the third day. You know, everyone's doing whatever the teacher said. I think instructions—when you're telling the students what to do—should definitely be in the target language. Some of the kids will pick up very quickly and then some will not. They'll kind of follow. They'll kind of look around and see what everybody else is doing. And, of course we as teachers, we're going to make some mistakes too, and most of the time the students won't know that we made the mistake. So it really doesn't matter. We know a heck of a lot more than they know. So if we tend to make a mistake or we forget a subjunctive, so "big deal," you know. The more you repeat and the more you repeat and the more you repeat, I think is so, so important.

T4: Well, . . . I agree with. You just have got to use the language constantly in class and then—go ahead and do it in the target language and then if it appears that they're totally lost, then stop and do it in English. But certainly give it a try [T1: Right.] in Spanish or in French or whatever first. And, you'll be surprised. I mean, they really do understand a lot more than you think they will, and there are lots of things that you can do to aid in their understanding. There are visuals that you can use. There are hand gestures or motions that you can use. There are . . . things that . . . you can make reference to. . . . It seems like I can remember in the article if they have something to pull from . . . Like if you're talking about a dog, for example, they know that the dog has four feet and that the dog needs to be fed, the dog needs to walk, and so forth. And so, if you're talking about a dog, they have some point of reference and so they're going to be anticipating some of that language anyway. And they can just . . . by anticipating, they can pick up on some things just by knowing a little. . . . If they can pick up on the main thing that you're talking about . . . [I: That's right.] but you have just got to use the language in class. Or, the students are never going to use it. . . . If you don't use it, if you don't model that and require that they speak to you in the target language all the time. . . . Then if you don't speak to them in the language all the time, then they're not going to. They're not going to ever learn to use the language themselves.

I: B.?

T3: The article mentioned something about attaching—how they attach meaning to words. And it has to have some real . . . I think it quoted, "real world connection." And I think the only way you're going to develop a real world connection is if you're using it in the real world. And show them that this is not just a code, this is not just something that somebody invented and it's not based on English. It can exist in and of itself as a means of communication. And, the more you use it and before long . . . I've seen my students . . . even they like . . . the French word *"avec"* which means "with." Some students have commented to me that they've been writing in English before and they'll suddenly write the word *"avec"* instead of the English word "with." And it's because you've just drilled it and you've just done it so many times. And I would say that the goal behind using the language in class is to get to the point where for instance: If we were having a class now and you are in and sat down and said, "OK, . . . turn to page thirty-nine. . . ." We wouldn't even think about [it] . . . all right, we would go like this. The goal is to be able to say that in the target language. And maybe, they didn't even realize you gave it to them in the target language.

T1: That's good.

T4: That is good. That is a good point.

T3: Right.

T1: And especially with numbers, because numbers are so, so difficult. If today you're on page five, tomorrow you're going to be on page six and the next day you'll be on page seven . . . and like you anticipate . . . and after a while, their numbers will come naturally. Yeah, that's a great point.

T4: And you just keep doing it day after day after day after day and it does get into that subconscious, so they don't have to think about it.

T3: I think some of the neatest experiences I've ever had in communicating in foreign language is: . . . I'll be talking to somebody and then you relate your friendship with this person to someone maybe in your family. And I'll call up my mother or something and say, "I have a friend who . . . this, this . . ." And then I'll have to stop and think, "Did they tell me that in French or in English, that they were going to be there tomorrow night and whatever time?" And then you don't know but you just know that it's tomorrow night at eight o'clock is when you're going to get together with the people—but you can't remember if they told you in French or English. I think that's the fun part.

T1: That's the ultimate goal [T4: It is. It is.] . . . the language. It has to be the ultimate goal. [I: Yeah, good.] You hope that, you know, a few of your students will reach that goal in your class.

I: In the article the author mentions that the input that we give, especially in the beginning level classes, should be simplified input—input that the students can understand. And he gave lots of examples on how to make that simple, with simple structure, with fewer pronouns, with simple verb tenses—so simplified. Do you do that consciously? Or does it just come to you naturally or do you do that at all when you . . . ? When you think about a first-year class and the first day of class, the first few weeks, and then you think that you have to speak in French or Spanish to them? Is there something that is set in your mind? "OK, I need to watch for how I use my French." Or . . . how do you do that?

T1: And again, like S. said earlier if you . . . if you're teaching a Level One class and you have to teach Level Two, Level Three, Level Four and even more than that through the day, you have to. You do simplify automatically and then, when you're still speaking French to them, you're using the vocabulary of the lesson. So, they know all this vocabulary and then you'll stick something in there that they'll know. You'll hear them. You'll see them. They'll know that you said something that they don't understand—that they haven't been taught yet. And then you say, "Oh, that's OK. We'll just go on and . . ." I think it comes naturally. You have to slow it down and you simplify it and make sure it's a subject, very, very simple object or . . .

T3: I remember a methods teacher once said in a class I was in . . . some philosophy where about 75 percent of your conversation should be things they already know. And then, this 25 percent is . . . you just constantly—that 25 percent just keeps moving along every day because you keep piling new stuff in that zone. And you link it—the 75 percent. Like everything you're saying is stuff of the lesson. And you say, "OK, this is French that I know they understand." And then, once you make them comfortable in that they're understanding, then you start giving them the new. And then you . . . they understand that new because it's linked to what they already know.

I: And that 25 percent, like you said, will become useful only just based on what they already know. Because if it's just too much beyond their heads it's just going to be useless.

T3: They have nothing to attach it to—"It's just a word" or "I have no clue what she said, or what he says."

I: Yeah. OK, in the article we have a section on second language acquisition and on how we process language. And the author mentions the
word "input" and then "intake." Input is what you give the students but
intake is what actually the students get and what the students will actually learn or process or understand. How do you see that happening
with your students?

T4: We do a lot of group work and so once they have the input part,
then they have to take whatever it is, whatever concepts or whatever
we're working on and work on that together in groups. And if they have,
if that intake has not taken place at that point, then they would not be
able to do that. So [I: That's a good example.] you're able to cruise
around the room and check with the different groups and see what's
going on. And they're pretty good about helping one another also. That's
one nice thing about that group work, I think is that they're able to feed
off one another. And if somebody has a weakness in an area then they'll
help one another with that. And so, in that way, they're getting intake.
They're getting that intake and sometimes they're getting input from one
another as well as input from the teacher—which I think really increases
their intake capabilities.

T1: Most definitely.

T4: Most definitely increases it. . . . We have groups of four and we also
have partners. And if they're getting from three other students in their
group it's more beneficial than just the teacher just standing up here, and
they're really learning a lot from each other.

T1: It really does reinforce.

T4: Plus, they're really getting to practice and use what they're doing,
so that intake that they've got is sealed, you know. [I: Exactly.] Once
they use it, then it becomes [I: Exactly. That's good . . .] a part of their
language.

T1: I use situation cards and they don't know what's on the card, and I
give them the card. It's in English. And there's a situation and then they
have to tell me what they're going to do in French. And I'll use maybe
four students at a time. And then, two or three days down the road, I'll
use another four students and to see if they've really kept that intake, if
it's really taken to their heads. And then, every once in a while, I'll go
back to three weeks ago and take out a situation card from three weeks
ago and see if they've still retained it. And that's when you really know
if they've really kept up with their vocabulary and their structure.

T3: See if the input really made it to intake.

T1: . . . really make it to intake and stay there. But I think any kind of
group work or partner . . . because they feel so much more comfortable
with their partner than you being the partner. [T4: They are.] Sometimes

you have to be the partner because you're initiating the questions, but it's just the best way, too. I think it's just the best way [T4: It is.] to work in a classroom. It gets a little noisy at times . . .

T3: That's why a language classroom is maybe a little bit more noisier than the average but they're learning to make good noise.

T1: That's right.

I: So imagine that you are working with a student teacher, with an intern now. And that student teacher tends to go back to English all the time. And they think again, the fear is that "the students will not understand me." Like that example that is in the book . . . that many teachers do believe that, and imagine if parents believe the same with the one-year-old kids, they will never be . . . children will never be able to learn any language. So the teacher—the first year teacher or the student teacher goes all the time back to English—giving commands in English in the class, explanations in English in the class. How would you convince that student not to do that?

T1: You're just going to have to make it a point to, when they come in, you know, it's "Hello" in the target language; it's "Let's review our homework from yesterday" in the target language; it's "What expressions did you learn last night when you did your homework?" in the target language. And insist . . . it just takes a day or two. Unless, you know, that student teacher is not confident enough to do that. Well then, that's another problem.

T4: I've tried with mine, when I've seen that happen to say to them, "I'm noticing that the students are speaking a lot of English. And I think that's probably because you are doing that, and . . . you need to be modeling what you want them to do." And they're speaking more English now. If you'll stop and think back to when you were sitting in and observing, how often were they speaking Spanish and how often were they speaking English? And, if you see that they're speaking a lot of English to you, it's probably because you are speaking a lot of English to them. And the only way you're going to get them to give Spanish back to you is if you're giving that input to them constantly and continually.

I: Now, the student may say to you, "But they don't understand me."

T4: But they will understand you . . . if you just hang in there and do it, they will understand you. They are going to understand. Model what you're doing. If you don't feel like they understand, have another student model what they're doing. If you feel like a particular student or group is not understanding, have them watch another student—what they're doing or what needs to be done in the exercise or whatever. Have them help one another if you feel like that's a problem. But you need to be speaking in the language.

I: Good. B.?

T3: Mine just goes back to . . . I hate to be repetitive but mine goes back to that seventy-five/twenty-five thing. I would say to the interns, "In doing that, you need to make, fill your lesson." I mean, even if the first part is just to use stuff that you know they know how, that they understand you. And then link it into this new. Of course, that's obviously easier said than done. I guess it's another one of these inexplicable things, that kind of thing that appears naturally, once you get in front of the classroom. It's kind of hard for me to express it in this setting, but it's something that you just kind of figure out. "OK, what can I do to make them get this point across, that I'm wanting to teach them today, you know, commands of 'get up,' 'raise your hand,' 'go to the door,' 'give me,' 'give the pencil to her.' " These would all be things that you would just have to model constantly and so that they have to get to apply meaning by seeing it in action. And then constantly hearing it so many times that . . . I mean, the only reason I know this is a pen is because somebody . . . kept saying "pen." And I eventually said "pen." "It must be a pen." So, you'll catch on and probably the baby didn't say "pen" the first two or three hundred times they heard it, probably. But they eventually got there. For quite a while now, I've known it's a pen.

I: Good, good. Another point that the article addresses is that input has to be comprehensible. We've talked about that and comprehensible and a little bit beyond—exactly what B. has been saying. And also, it says that input has to be meaning-bearing, meaning that it has to be of some interest, of some meaning to the students. Why do you think that is so important?

T1: More applicable to their daily life. You're going to, when you teach reflexive verbs, when that concept of reflexive verb that we don't really have in English. . . . You're not going to talk about—I can think of an example of . . . What would be a reflexive verb that you don't use everyday? You're going to use, you know, "What did you do this morning before you came to school?" "Well, I got up. I really didn't want to, but I got up and I went to the bathroom and I washed my face and I brushed my teeth and . . ." And then, what I usually tell them with reflexive verbs, "Now, tonight, when you do all these things, tell yourself what you're doing. Make it applicable so it's . . . vocabulary you use every single day." You know, and it has to apply. It can't be meaningless.

T4: In Spanish, for example, some of the reflexive verbs like "*darse cuenta*" means "to realize." [T1: That's hard.] I mean, that probably in Level One and Level Two would be something that you would not work with, even though that's a reflexive verb. You know, because they're going to use that when they get in Level Three and Level Four. [T1: Right.] But, I agree with S., you have got to make it things that they do.

"When do you get up in the morning?" "Well, I get up at eight o'clock." "Well, when do you get up in the morning?" "Oh, you get up really early. Why do you get up so early?" And then, they're talking about things that matter to them. They're not going to remember it if it doesn't matter to them or if it has no application to their lives or to anything that affects them. You have to use those things that have meaning to them. If you're talking about, well you know, "Do you realize that it's . . . almost the year 2000?" . . . That's not a concept that in Level One or Level Two you're going to want to get to.

T3: I would say, you're going to have to ask yourself, "Is what I'm teaching them today something that they can actually go out of here from this classroom and would actually, possibly . . . they might encounter the need to actually say this today." I doubt that they would go off and need to say in Spanish, "I realize that I . . ." You know, like you said, you know those teeth are probably going to get brushed before bed that night. And you know that the television is going to be watched and you know the homework is going to be done. And, you know that this and this and this is going to happen. So flood them with vocabulary you know they can use and that they will use and . . . I love what you said. Tell them to use it. I tell my students, "Go on. Close the door if you're embarrassed but go in your room and just start speaking French to yourself. Go through, tell yourself in French, 'What are you doing right now?' 'I'm taking my books out of my book bag.' 'I'm writing.' 'I'm doing my homework.' 'I am tired.' And that's the only way that you're going to do it."

T1: That's the only way that you can practice: "I am this. I am that." And you know, "Which one do I refer, use for this? Well I'm tired, so it's got to be . . ." And you know, make it [T4: Meaningful.] fun, too. Make it meaningful. Tell them to talk to their friends. You know, I have them call each other on the telephone. You know, just things like that, at the One level. I love to teach French One.

T4: If I come in and I say, "Well, my daughter graduated from Carolina and then I have another daughter who attends NC State." And some of them are going to be attending universities soon, so they're interested in that automatically—Whereas if I just pick up a picture and show them a family, and say they have two older daughters and they go to where-ever . . . [T1: Who cares?] and they don't care about that. . . . Or if I know about some of their families and I talk about their own family and say, you know, "Well, he has two brothers and I taught his older brother and I know his older brother. His brother's name is John, and I taught him several years ago. And he's now at Wilmington studying whatever." Then they're interested in that because they're people that they know or people that they connect with.

T1: It has to be real. You have to make your classrooms just as real because as I mentioned last time, they are still not sure that this language will work, you know—that it is a real thing. You know, they're really not quite sure at the beginning. "Can I take these words and when I go to France and use them . . ." You know, so you have to really use really good real situations to make it more real than . . .

T4: I like to get them to talk about five minutes at the beginning of every class just about whatever may be going on. This week we've talked about Homecoming because that's what's going on in our school this week. When they come in on Monday, I'm going to ask them what they did on the weekend. And I'm going to expect them to be able to tell me the activities that they attended and the things that they did. And they want to talk about what they did. So they're going to want to raise their hands and tell, you know, tell me and the rest of the class what they did on the weekend. And that makes it, that makes it more fun. Or, if we come in on a Monday and everybody's tired and "blah" and you know, I ask them how they feel. "Well, why are you tired? What is it you've done that's made you tired?" And then they can really get into, you know, talking about that. Or they went to a movie. "Well, what movie did you see?" And then we can talk about those movies. And they get interested in talking about that because it is things they are interested in. But you are using that vocabulary all the time.

I: But it's interesting and fun, so the two are together. Any other thoughts about this article? Or the other one by Krashen? Or on input and the importance of . . . ? How do you balance the use of the target language and English? When do you use English in the class?

T1: It really depends . . .

T4: You use it when you absolutely have to [T1: Yeah.] basically.

T1: Because when you're going to try to teach something that's brand new . . . let's say direct object pronouns. Well, they're really . . . you can do that in French. You know, you can have your subject, verb, and your direct object and then you can take your direct object. And I use colors and I use, you know, your subject and numbers this color and your verbs this color and your direct objects are green and your indirect objects are blue. Well, you take the noun that's blue but then you can put it before the verb if it's a pronoun. And you can do things. [I: Visually.] You can do things and then, if you see they are really not understanding, then you say, "OK, well let's do it in . . ." But try it [T3: Yes . . .] especially at the One and Two level . . . it's not so complex.

T3: I probably have yet to have ever talked the first day of the subjunctive in the target language.

I: You have or you haven't?

T3: No, I probably haven't because I've often. . . . You find yourself immediately going into English to explain the abstract idea.

T1: Like imperfect and preterit. . . . You can work at it, but then you might lose a few and then you might have to say, "OK, I think we've got to do this [T4: In English.] in English."

T4: But you should try. [T1: Yeah.] You should try and then do examples and if you see that you're, that they're not getting it then go to your English. But you should . . . even things that you think might not . . . like the subjunctive, you know. I do introduce the subjunctive in the target language usually. I may go back the second day and do it in English and just reinforce that. But I'll start with Spanish and you know—illustrations and things on the board or things on an overhead and you can get those points across.

I: Good. Any other thought about input? So this also brings us to the importance of the student teachers knowing the language so well. Because if you do not know the language you cannot become confident enough to use the target language in the classroom.

T1: Because if you have to think about what you're saying and then translate it in your head and then give it to the kids. . . . It might take a few seconds there and then they see you pause and it's got to be spontaneous, you know. . . .

T3: I think that takes away from what we were talking about earlier—the realness of it [T1: Right.] that the students may begin to question, "Is it real for you?" [T1: Right.] [I: That's right.] [T1: You really have to be right.] And it's funny how that seems to be a continual foundation of everything . . . everything we've seemingly talked about in this group, if the student—if the intern does not know the language, then, it's like . . . we're building the house without the foundation.

T4: Right. Exactly. And in order to be really confident in the language, you really do need to be somewhere in that culture, some period of time—if it's only a month, you know, if it's a couple of weeks or whatever. But you really, you really do need to travel, guys.

T4: Yes, you really do.

SESSION #3

I: Today we are going to discuss your best activities to teach reading, listening, grammar and vocabulary, etc., or, and writing probably, too.

T1: OK, all right . . .

I: S., you want to start?

T1: I'm going to explain an activity I do with my advanced class, my AP class. Usually on Mondays, every Monday I start with a song. And they get an exercise, and I've got some writing on here but you can't really see it from there. But, they get a song that relates to a current event that we have been discussing. And this current event is the Referendum—the Quebec Referendum that's coming up in the next year. . . . Three years ago the Referendum almost passed that Quebec was going to separate from the rest of Canada. And, they are thinking now that this year they will separate. And so, the prime minister who is a Quebecqua used to be a separatist. He doesn't doubt that this will happen, so the song is. . . . We've talked about the problem in Quebec and the Quebecqua want to preserve the language. French is very dear to them and they don't want anything English in their culture. And so, this song is a song by [a man] who is probably in his late sixties. He's a folk artist and he talks about his land and of course he is for the separation of Quebec and for the preservation of the language and the culture and the French roots. And so, they listen to the song and then they have to for listening comprehension, they have to fill in the words that are missing. And they're good vocabulary words. They're words that deal with what we've been talking about. And, after we've listened to it a couple or three times, we'll talk about the message, the moral. They have to keep a vocabulary notebook in AP. . . . Their notebook is almost full and we're only nine weeks already into the year. But they're responsible for any grammar that we talk about in this song. So . . . You really incorporate a lot of things, but the primary object is for the listening comprehension . . .

I: How many times do they listen to the song?

T1: They'll listen to it no more than three times. After three times, they feel they know all the words. [I: OK.] And if then there's a word that they can't get, they will talk about it or I'll give it to them or something like that. But they love this activity. It could be a long song, a short song. They know that on Mondays they're expecting a song and they really like it.

I: What do they do after they fill out the blanks? Do they sing the song?

T1: If they want to, yeah. I can't sing so I don't make them sing. But sometimes I'll hear them sing the refrain. It's a very melodious song and they'll sing. They'll come in the next day and sing a little bit and so, you know, I know that's it's in there.

I: So every Monday?

T1: I try to do it every Monday. I went to an AP workshop a couple of years ago and the woman who did the AP workshop sold a cassette with song activities. I've used a couple of hers. Some of them are a little complicated. A lot of them are love songs. So, you know, they're not really appropriate. They gave me an idea about this song which is a popular folk song in France that all little children know and adults know. And it has a lot of double-object pronouns in it, so I plan to do that next week because we're reviewing pronouns next week. So, anything that I can find ... I'm going to use a lot of Celene Dion's French songs. I've got two or three that I plan to use. And just to expose [them] to different cultural songs, I think. And you could probably find the songs that are easy that you could use at the One, Two, Three, Four Level, you know. I do that in AP a lot. It's good for listening-comprehension. So, that's my listening activity. I don't know if it's the best. I mean, we do listening activities all day long, you know. Either they listen to you or they listen to themselves or they listen to the tape [T4: The tape.] or we sometimes ... I know S. probably does this. We make our own tapes with certain exercises and let them do it without repetition. Because in the classroom you tend to repeat and repeat until they get it—until you feel they've gotten it. But then sometimes you want them to listen to it once and see if they get it. And that's good. That's good to build the skills.

I: Do you do anything in particular to prepare them for the song? Like any pre- ... ?

T1: It all depends on what we've talked about. Any pre-listening? I don't think so. [I: No?] No, no.

I: Like just the preparation would be the discussion?

T1: The discussion ... we didn't do pre-listening.

I: OK. Do you normally do pre-listening when you do listening activities? For Level One, and Two, probably more than Level Three?

T1: Probably so, yeah. I think you have to.

I: Why do you think it is important—the pre-listening?

T1: Well, so that they can first of all know what to expect. Second of all, acclimate their ear to the subject that they're going to hear.

I: OK, good. OK, S.?

T4: I have a similar activity that I do and I really like songs because I feel like kids are more likely to listen than if you just do a speaking-listening activity. And I did the same thing. I attended a workshop a number of years ago and got a cassette tape that someone was selling that has songs on it that illustrate various grammar points. And the songs ... there's a song using the subjunctive which is a difficult concept to grasp. And I do listening-comprehension with that after we have studied the subjunctive, so that would really be the part. And this would be in Spanish Level Three. And basically what I do is very similar to that where you would have the song with blanks in it and . . . we listen and they have to fill in the blanks. And I think that's a wonderful activity to do with songs.

I: Do you do any kind of listening activity in which they have to mainly pay attention to the message? To the content?

T4: Yes. That wouldn't necessarily be something that I would do in a song because these songs that I have are related to grammar issues. But we have a number of good, good listening activities that actually come with our textbook. And so we listen to a lot of tapes and when we listen to the tape, I may give them a statement about generally what it's about. We'll listen to it one time. Kind of let them internalize it for a few minutes. I'll rewind it. We'll listen to it again. Then, I will ask oral questions about it sometimes. Sometimes we'll do written questions. It depends on what we're doing at the time. And all of our tests include listening comprehension. All of them include listening-comprehension.

I: Why is it important for you to have the pre-listening?

T4: To prepare them for what . . . I mean, just to give them a total "abstract something" out of nowhere with no idea of what it's about—I really think "throws" them. It prepares them for what they're going to be hearing. It helps them to "zero-in" maybe on what their focus should be as they're listening.

I: Do you have any examples of the types of pre-listening activities, besides your telling the students about the general idea of the text?

T4: Well, in some of the activities that actually go along with the textbook, there are actual activities that go before the listening sections. That would be more than just my giving them a brief statement about it. And it might be something cultural that they would read about. And depending on what level it is, that little reading might be in English or it might be in Spanish depending on what, which level book it's in. It might be something cultural. It might be just a discussion in English about something similar, maybe to get them think along those lines. There's lots of different activities.

T3: Is that like a listening-comprehension thing on a test? [I: No.] Is that what you're . . . ?

I: This is teaching listening-comprehension. The test would be a different story, because you would play it once and without the pre-preparation, because it's a test.

T3: I like to write stories based on vocabulary. That's a little more work for me. And I don't need to sit home and practice it because I know the vocabulary . . . I've got the pages memorized. I go around on test day and tell them, "That was on page ninety-two." In fact, I just did that in fourth period just a little while ago. This girl asked me, "What does that mean?" I said, "I can't tell you that . . ." But anyway, I love to go write stories and use the vocabulary from the current section. And I've got a bunch of them that I have written myself.

I: Now you have to bring them to me.

T3: I know. I will.

I: Yeah, that would be nice.

T3: And what I do is I write the story at home on my computer and I make the font big and bold. And I then I take it to school and put it on a transparency and put it on the overhead. And then, the students read the story. Sometimes I'll read it once, then other students will read it. I'll say, "I want you to read it first, sentence by sentence. And somebody else volunteer to read the whole second paragraph by yourself." And then, once we've gotten the whole gist of the story in French. . . . Before-hand, I have developed a list of true-false questions about the story—or statements. And I go to the tape recorder in my classroom and I tape my own voice on the recorder. And what I'll do is I'll deepen my voice a little bit and . . . it comes out on a tape and invariably, every time I've done it, some kid has asked me, "Is that you? Or is that somebody else?" But I think even if it is my voice, it's coming from a different source and it's requiring them to focus in somewhere else and hear French. And so, we've read the story about whoever doing whatever and then I start saying, "All right. I want to know . . ." or ". . . " and then "Just write it on your scrap sheet of paper." I'm forever telling them, "Pull out a scrap sheet of paper for the listening-comprehension stuff." And then, they just whip that little piece of paper out . . .

I: And the "true or false" is with the listening only, not reading?

T3: No, well, they've read the story and they've heard the story [I: To-gether.] together. And then they hear, they only hear the statement and they've got to think back and remember. "Did he go to the café? No he ordered something else. And so . . . I enjoy doing it because they enjoy it. I also like to write stories and come to a place where I have paren-theses. And I make the parentheses and the two words within the pa-rentheses in italics. And so we'll be going along and "boom." They've got to choose: "Which one of these two words is naturally going to fall next?"

I: And you do that more for reading?

T3: That would probably be more for reading. Of course we read it aloud though, so they're hearing it, too. But I like to do things like that.

T1: I like that true-false idea because a lot of oral listening-comprehension on the tests—on the chapter tests—they'll give you a little conversation. Well, it's not little. Even at Level One, they'll give you a conversation that long at the café. And you've got to figure out, "Well, who ordered what?" And of course I allow them to . . . they can write anything they want. And they hear. And, that would be good practice because once they hear that sentence, they only hear it once. They've got to decide and that's hard.

T4: It is hard.

T1: It's hard. It's good practice.

T3: I did a unit on the family recently. And one of the things that I did . . . and I hadn't even planned to test them this way, but they enjoyed it so much I ended up doing the test like this. I gave them a family tree with a list of names underneath it and I put in one name. And then I started saying on a tape, saying aloud, " 'Such and such' is 'such and such's' brother." And then, they have to put it in the right spot. And it totally requires them to listen.

T1: . . . to do that.

T3: I enjoy that.

T1: And we're just finishing that in Level One—the family tree.

I: That is neat.

T1: I do that. It's a great exercise.

I: One more point that you mentioned is letting the student listen to the tape more than once and that . . . you ask "Is this testing or teaching?" Why is it important in teaching to let them listen to the material more than once?

T1: Well, it will stay with them longer. They will catch things that they didn't catch the first time. I think the more they listen, the better off they are. It'll stick with them.

T4: I think a listening skill is almost like . . . listening to language is almost like listening to music. You know, the more you do it, the more your ear is tuned for it, you know. People who are really adept in music, it's because they've listened a lot. And, people who understand language have listened a lot. And so, the more you do, the more you are tuning that ear. That ear is practicing to hear and to understand. In the Level Two book, we have sections called *Aqui Escuchamos.* . . . And the text is actually written in the book. We will listen to the tape and they will look at it. They'll get to read along with it. Then we'll close the books and listen to it again. Then I'll rewind the tape and we'll listen to it one more time, and then I will ask them questions about it. So they've really had it one time seeing it and twice hearing it so they can really pick up on what they need to.

T1: And at the beginning it's going to be a lot of memory work. It's almost like they've memorized. They've repeated it so much that they've memorized it but at the same time, they know what they're saying. You know, I tell them, "I don't care if you memorize as long as you comprehend what you memorize." And then, after that, it becomes knowledge. [I: That's right.] You know, it's not just memory work just for this activity and then after you're through, you forget it. So the more they repeat the better off they are.

T3: And you've got to incorporate what they did in the previous units into the new—not let it go away.

T1: Sometimes that's hard to do.

T3: Yeah, very hard to do. I tell them, "Algebra and French have a lot in common. You learned the multiplication tables in the third grade and you're still needing to know them, aren't you? And you learned [it] way back there, but see, it's forever popping it's little head up." . . . forever needing to know it . . . it just doesn't disappear like history maybe, where you finish the Civil War, then you go to Reconstruction and then World War I. And then, you don't need to know the Civil War anymore, but . . .

I: But when they are in the comprehension part of the listening activity, do you let them read over the questions, or the "true or false" statements, or the charts that they have to fill out before they listen to the tape or after? Or during?

T4: It varies. It really varies. I mean, sometimes it's one way and sometimes it's another way. On most of our tests, the listening-comprehension sections—they see the questions as they are listening. [I: On the test?] . . . In other words, they're written right on the test and they see them. So they know what they're listening for but they're only going to hear it once. So sometimes . . . depending on what the activity is, I might give them a minute before I start the tape to just look over that, so they're not having to read at the same time. You know, that they're trying to listen and . . . but most of the time with practice . . . like when you're teaching, they don't see those things ahead of time.

I: They don't. Any reason?

T4: Well, I think you're practicing, you know. And plus, the fact that they're getting their listening more than one time—whereas with the test they're only getting that one . . . [I: One time.] that one time. So when they're practicing, I don't know that they need it so much, because they are getting . . . they are hearing it.

I: Any other responses?

T1: I tend to agree with S. Although on tests, in our textbook, they don't see it. They don't see the question [I: Before.] beforehand.

I: Any other response?

T3: I'm lost for words. I don't have anything to add right now.

I: OK. Do you do anything . . . ? When we talk about teaching listening skills, we talk about post-listening—what they do after they have listened. After they have done the "true or false" or the charts or the questions or whatever. Post-listening, which is in a way relating what they have listened to to their own lives. Do you do any kind of that post-listening?

T1: You mean after they've listened and we've talked about the song? You know, "How would this affect you if you were to live in Quebec? How would you feel?" Yeah, we do that all the time. Yeah, that's very important. . . . You're kind of wrapping up your lesson and your cultural unit and whatever you've been talking about. . . . Sure, we're going to ask the questions after we've used the subjunctive. You know, "What are some of the things that you must do?" And "Are you upset that the new regulations have been imposed on high school students?" I mean, all that uses the subjunctive. Sure, you're going to . . . you have to make the language real. You have to talk about things that either you've been discussing in the classroom in your particular unit or everyday things that you're going to use—these grammatical terms or these feelings . . . that's very important.

I: Any specific structures or exercises like . . . one would be discussing their own beliefs about certain topics . . . ?

T1: "Get with your partner and discuss something." I do that a lot, or maybe a writing activity after the discussion's been done or a lot of things. . . . [I: Good.] But that's very important.

I: Any other idea on the post-?

T4: I would just agree with what S. said, you know. And we do a lot of partner or group things to wrap up.

I: Any other reason why it is important?

T1: Well, it makes the subject applicable to their daily life and they need to be able to talk about that in French.

I: The most important . . .

T3: Sometimes it's good to take something that they've done and let them rephrase it so that it's applicable to them. For instance, . . . once they've seen the story about Jean Luc going to the café, then you can step back and ask them, "OK, how many of you are really probably going to need to go to France and talk about Jean Luc going to the café?" Not too many. But you're probably going to use a lot of ingredients here, and from this story, if you were to ask somebody about a café—or if you were to tell somebody what you did or what you would like to do. And so, now,

". . . I want you to rewrite this, using this maybe as a model, but now make it real to you. What would you order if you had been there? What would have done if this had happened? Jean Luc did this. Would you have done the same thing? When the woman dropped her food, he cried out . . . Would you have done the same thing? Or would you have done something different? Make it applicable. Make it real to you."

I: Good. Any other idea on listening? OK, thank you very much. . . . Reading? Similar process? Before we go into reading, something that also, when we talk about teaching listening or reading, theory stresses the importance of using authentic material—like a song or a video, or interesting to the students? Why is that important? When you read about it, you read the word "authentic" all the time versus "unrealistic" or "uninteresting" or "disconnected to anybody's life"? Why is the use of authentic material or interesting material very important?

T4: Because if it's not authentic, they're not going to internalize anything. They're not going to, they're not really going to get anything from it. It's just going to be an exercise and then it's gone. And so, it's really useless to them. But if it's something authentic . . . if you've taken it from a magazine, if you're singing a song, if you're reading about something cultural that you're studying right now. Then . . . if you're reading about Flamenco and then we watch someone dance it and then we listen to a guitarist, then it's real to them and they're going to remember it.

I: Good. Any other ideas?

T1: I agree. If it's real, they'll remember it and ten years down the road, they'll remember that from this class.

T4: They will. [I: Good.]

T3: They won't just consider it something they got written for them to use in that classroom.

T1: That's right.

T3: They'll say, "How, this is really happening somewhere in the world." I guess that's where sometimes the internet can be as useful. You can tap into some resources from different languages and say, "This is coming directly from France right now. And let's read this news story. And what's happening in the Paris suburbs today . . . ? They had something happen big here. They're having a strike about this. What are they striking for? . . ."

I: Let's talk about reading? Share your best.

T4: Well, I have this great little sheet that I'll give you a copy of, that I like to use.

I: Good.

T4: And it's strategies for reading comprehension.

I: Good.

T4: It's things like . . . I'll just read you some of the topics: "Knowledge of the World," "Recognize Cognates and Borrowed Words," "Skim for the Main Ideas," "Scan for Specific Information," "Guess a Meaning from Context," "Identify Who, What, When, Where, Why" (all the "W's"), and then just some other little strategies: "Look at Word Families and Parts of Speech," "Word Formation," "Chronological Information," and so forth. And this is "Using the Dictionary Effectively," and so forth . . . it's a good tool. You can use it at an any level. You can use it for Level One.

I: So the students get a copy?

T4: Yes, yes, the students get a copy. You can use this for Level One all the way through advanced. By the time they get to an advanced class, they already have a lot of these skills, but I talk with students about reading constantly—about cognates and word families. "What does that word look like?" and "Can you relate that to anything else?" Because that is such an important skill for reading. That is so very, very important. But anyway, you can have a copy of that.

I: Good.

T4: You can have that too if you want it.

T1: *Gracias.* I think we all do the same things as far as pre-reading activities, because they're so important and if you have a long word, like ". . ." and the word "su" on the inside then the family relationship is there. And then they have to work at it. It's not easy. It's not easy at all; and we do a lot of exercises like that—a lot of dictionary exercises.

I: And that is like the pre-reading activity, you think?

T1: Well sometimes it's pre-reading. Sometimes if they have a lot of new vocabulary work in the reading assignment you have to study beforehand. Then you can talk about the cognates then, but then sometimes you might be reading together in class or with a partner, and then I tell them to try and figure it out through context of sentence before they raise their hand and say, "We really don't understand it." I guess it can be pre-reading or during the activity . . .

T3: I've found the textbook that I'm using now to be helpful with reading, pre-reading, and ideas on the side. Of course you don't rely on the textbook all the time, but the teacher's edition of this edition has given some good things for the reading sections at the end of each chapter. They tell you some things to suggest—suggested things to do before they read the passage.

I: Some examples?

T3: Some things have already been said: scan for cognates, what do you think is going on, different little ideas. My mind goes blank, but it's not long ago I asked them, "OK, based on the words you can pick out, what do you think this story is going to be discussing? You can recognize these two words from this paragraph. You recognize this so you know . . . suddenly we're predominately talking about food; that is part of the paragraph." You get a pretty good idea what it is talking about.

I: Do you do anything with titles or pictures together with the text, if they are together with the text?

T4: Did you say titles?

I: Titles, subtitles, or pictures . . . how do you use them?

T4: Well, I can think right off the top of my head a reading we had in the Spanish 3 book which was about fashion, and the pictures on the page were of someone in a vest. The reading was about how Spanish clothing was influenced by the gypsies and the Gypsy Kings who were very, very popular musicians. And so it goes into Gypsy Kings and their influence in the south of Spain, and how that's affected clothing and so forth. The picture on the page is a vest, which is a gypsy thing, and on the other side of the page a guitar. Gypsy Kings are there and the page just has this on the background of the reading. That's a wonderful way! Just a glance of what they're seeing lets them know a lot of what they're going to be reading.

I: How do you use the pictures?

T4: We might talk about them before we even start the reading and "Does that mean anything to you, do you recognize who this group is?" We might even listen to some Gypsy Kings music before we even do the reading so they'll know who the Gypsy Kings are—we might pull out a map and talk about Andalusia and the relevance of gypsies in the region. We would do all that before ever doing the reading so they'll have some of that background knowledge. The pictures are a great way of leading into that and discussing.

I: Any other ideas on pictures or anything graphic you might see?

T1 : I think pictures are important if they go along with the text. In Level One we're using very elementary, simple reading, talking about the southern part of France. Of course there were lavender fields on the background of the text and we can talk about the perfumery and how that's an important industry. I think pictures are important and the kids like them too.

I: And you?

T3: Nothing in addition.

T4: Some of the exercises actually before the reading will have an activity to go through and pick out the cognates you know. Go through and make a list of all the cognates so that before they even do that reading there are a lot of things they are going to know.

I: That's important.

T4: For example, the weather. If you have a reading on weather, it's going to be absolutely full of cognates. And it amazes them they can read something like that and understand it because there are so many cognates. And it's wonderful they can have something like that and have success with that because of word families and cognates.

I: Anything about reading that we haven't said before when we talk about listening? But they are quite similar skills. More or less the same pattern? Do you usually make them read out loud in class?

T4: Sometimes.

I: What would be the difference between silent reading and reading out loud?

T4: Reading out loud to me, I think, is the same in any language. Or reading silently. Sometimes you want to read to yourself but sometimes it's easier to understand if you hear it. Plus they're also getting pronunciation practice by doing that, and sometimes you have one person read a paragraph or do the popcorn thing. Each person reads a sentence and we'll go around. Or sometimes we'll do it in groups or pairs and when you do it in groups and pairs, everyone has the opportunity to actually do the reading. I know it helps if I'm reading. I'd rather read something out loud than silently. I think you concentrate and comprehend better.

T3: And especially at the level where they are, I mean, if you're talking about Level One, some of them may not have the ability to read it silently and really catch the meaning. I have trouble in English. I have to say things out loud sometimes in English. I have to say, "Wait a minute, I have no clue what I just read." (murmurs of assent from other teachers) I think hearing is good. I tell my students, I say, "Listen, if all you do is look at something, one area of your brain has been engaged: the visual center. But if you will read it, listen to it, say it, and write it, that's four areas of your brain [that] have been involved in learning that particular word or unit or group of words. You're much more likely to remember, to have it up there somewhere and be able to use it than if all you did was look at it." I tell them to write the vocabulary—go home and just start writing it. And for those kids who are having trouble remembering to spell—their spelling is just atrocious sometimes, and they ask you on the test, "Are you going to take off for spelling?" And then I'll say, "Well, I may let a few things slide, but if you were to spell 'apple' 'o-r-a-n-g-e,' that I'm going to take off."

I: Good example.

T4: That is a good example.

T3: She saw my class—she saw J. My favorite student, J.

I: Yeah, great. Anything else for reading? No? OK, good. Grammar, vocabulary?

T4: Grammar? OK.

T1: I'll start with grammar.

I: OK.

T1: This is a student activity, is that okay? We have worked and reviewed the use of the *"imparfait"* and the *"passé composé,"* maybe this is a writing activity. . . . I like to introduce at the One Level vocabulary and grammar together. And, at the beginning, they don't know that they've learned grammar. I don't like to teach vocabulary in isolation. It's not very meaningful to me, and it's not very meaningful to them. We do the family tree with a transparency—a lot of times I introduce new vocabulary on the overhead—but we talk about Monique or anybody in the classroom, and *"Monique a un frère,"* she has a brother, and we learn the vocabulary and learn also the verb "to have" which is introduced in this chapter. We even introduce the plural of "have"—"the grandparents have two children"—so they know that the plural of "have" is the "ont." They have no idea how to spell it, but they may have an inclination on how to spell it, they can say it, and we have repeated it and repeated it, so I like to incorporate the grammar with the vocabulary—whatever grammar it is.

I: Do you go at one point into explaining rules, or . . . ?

T1: No rules! No rules, we just talk about it. And then we go into the "you" and the "I" form. "Do you have a brother," ask your partner if he has a brother, and say, "No, I don't have a brother." So, we've included "avoir"—the verb "to have"—and we've negated, and we ask a question, *"Est-ce que tu as un frère?"* And we do that for quite some time, with this particular lesson. So we've learned the members of the family, the verb "to have," negating it, asking questions, and there's a little preposition, another grammar point, when you negate, you don't say "I don't have a brother," you say, "I don't have *de frères,"* and so, that's something that is important if you want to speak correctly. So, I like to do that.

I: So all of that is listening, they don't see any words, right?

T1: They don't see any words. But you know if we do it we talk about "fraternity," and we have *"frères,"* and "sorority" and we have *"soeurs,"* and *"mère"* and "maternal" and *"père"* and "paternal."

I: When do they see the written words?

T1: When they're asked to go home and learn them.

I: As homework.

T1: It's in their book—and they learn it—and if they can't remember the pronunciation, "Well how did we say that in class, how did we say this with this overhead?" and they get the pronunciation pretty quickly.

I: Any reason—the philosophy behind that?

T1: I think they better understand what they're doing—if they learn it at first, why learn the word for mother and father and not put it into a sentence that they can apply it? And use it with their partner, right away? You know, I . . . even going back to our subjunctive, at Level One they know how to say, "I've got to go to the bathroom," [which is] "*Il faut que j'aille aux toilettes.*" So they know to use the subjunctive at the beginning, they don't know what it is!

T3: Probably haven't even noticed you said it.

T1: They don't know what this is, but . . .

I: But it works better.

T1: For me it does, and I think for them it does.

I: Good.

T1: And so . . .

T4: But that is at Level One?

T1: That is at Level One.

T4: You're talking . . . of course . . .

T1: Oh, yeah.

T4: You do have to get into grammar explanations with . . .

T1: Oh, sure. And you even will have to get into grammar explanation—but when you can do it that way it works. I think it works better.

T3: I agree.

T1: To incorporate the new grammar and vocabulary at the same time.

I: It's usually much more interesting.

T1: Yeah. And our text does it. They'll have . . . (picks up overhead sheet) and this is the picture that they see in their text. But they will see the words, and they might have a sentence over here to the side. . . . "Monique's brother is Phillipe," and "Phillipe is fourteen years old," and then there's another grammar point, so they'll see that in their text, they incorporate the grammar and the vocabulary together, too.

I: Any other ideas about teaching grammar?

T4: I'm like S., I like . . . any way you can find to incorporate it with other things and again, make it authentic, that we just have to keep going back to that word because that's just so important—the last unit that we did in Spanish III was on foods—and we did, actually we did one chapter on Spanish foods. Foods from Spain, and then one on Latin American foods, that's in our text book, but one of the grammar points in that chapter was the impersonal "se": one does this, you do this, they do this, and so, since we were doing foods, I had them do recipes—using that grammar point.

I: Wow . . .

T4: So, this is a recipe for *"licuados"* and they had to write a little bit about the recipe—the origin of it, give the ingredients, and then the steps of preparation, and in the steps of preparation, they had to use that impersonal "se" form . . . this is one on *"frijoles negros,"* same type of thing, the paragraph, the ingredients, and then the steps of preparation and in the steps of preparation they had to use that "se" form. So as many authentic ways as you can find . . . to say, "This is how this would be used," then the more likely. And of course any time you touch the palate, you touch their hearts too. And of course they prepared these foods, besides doing this recipe they prepared these foods and each person had to do their recipe like this, so . . .

I: How would you teach that same form the first time—"se"?

T4: Well, I'll give you a copy of those, . . . the textbook has a lot of good exercises where you just simply start, *"¿Cómo se dice? ¿Qué se habla en España?"* You know, if, the more examples you can give with conversation then you get into the book and do exercises with it, then you have, of course I have an example from our workbook where they actually have written exercises with the grammar point also, and then of course the culminatory thing is to pull it together and do it themselves, in something that is authentic.

I: Good, so you will keep the explanations to the minimum.

T4: And of course, this is a fairly easy point, too. If you're doing subjunctive, you know, then obviously you can't keep the explanation to a minimum. But, so it depends on what you're teaching. But with this particular point which we just finished doing, that's a pretty easy concept, and we'll do things like, you know, how do you set the table? And we'll actually have people get up and set the table, *"Se pone el plato en el centro"* and using that "se" form, so there's many different ways that we'll practice using that before writing it and then pulling it together into something authentic.

T3: I like to teach grammar in any way I can get it across! . . . but I agree that the best way is to incorporate it in whatever you're doing so you just don't sit there and make them—and I'm not saying that I do this, but you just don't sit up there and explain in English, "Oh, you drop

this and you do this and you do this, here's a worksheet—go do it." . . .
They've got to see it in action.

I: What is wrong with that?

T3: It's not real. I will say that I have had some students for whom—
they got to the point that that way is the only way they could learn, is
when you really sat down with it, because they were just not getting it
in class. And you had to break it down. You had to get beside them after
school, and say, "All right, this is what you do now, you gotta drop that
"-er," that's gotta get outta here." And then you have to just sit there
and explain it to them. But your first initial approach needs to be, perhaps, let them see it being used first, and then break down into the
intricate details if needed, and a lot of times they'll pick up on the details
(snaps fingers). They'll realize that in the "-er" verb when "tu" is the
subject, they're going to add an "s" on the end of it without thinking
about it.

I: Just because they've seen it?

T3: Just because they've seen it. And so, well, every time we've done
that, it always has an "s" on the end and so then, sometimes before you
even get to the explanation about conjugating "-er" verbs, they already
know that it's going to have an "s." Sometimes I'll tell them, "You tell
me now how to do it. You go up and explain it." I love to make students
go up and teach.

T1: I do that, too. Just to make sure now, in English, you explain to the
class exactly this concept that we just learned, you explain to the class,
to your classmate just to make sure that we all understand it. That helps.

T3: The first night of every French I class I teach (this is the second year
in a row I've done it), their first night's homework is they have a sheet
of paper and it's a thing that they have to get their parents to sign it and
they get a free daily grade of 100 percent if they bring it back the next
day signed by their parent and it's a little thing that says, "My son or
daughter, Johnny or Lucy, taught me everything he learned in class today, including dadada, etc." signed by the parent. And I tell them, one
of the best ways to study is to teach it to someone at home. Because if
you can teach it, you truly know it. I learned more French than I ever
thought I would.

I: Neat . . . great ideas. Terrific that you are here. Anything else for grammar? Vocabulary? You have said something about it. Anything else
about teaching vocabulary?
[Participants notice a handout on weather.]

T4: But, you know, if you're going to teach weather, just start out by
putting the overhead up, and to maybe talk about the weather last week.
Even though it may be past tense, you're still getting the vocabulary in,

or what it's like today, or what it's going to be like tomorrow and using pictures of what things you do when the weather is a certain way and . . . here's the actual vocabulary page. (Holds up page with vocabulary words on it, juxtaposed with the handout with pictures.) You know, I mean, booooring. That's, you know, to just look at that. But this is so much better, to have this on overhead, to make it authentic, and "What do you like to do when it rains?" "What's a good activity . . . when it's snowing?" . . . anything that you can do to involve them in it, and again, I love singing, and so for something like this, I'll teach them a song with the seasons, with the months of the year, or something. Days of the week, or, this particular unit has weather, . . . so we'll also do songs because I feel like with a song, even though they act like they absolutely hate it, they really do like it. And they remember so much better. And if you go back and ask them something they've done in a song, it comes right back to them, because . . . if they get the melody, they get the words back and so they will remember it so much better. But, you just have got to make it authentic—I was away for two days, so what I asked the students was, it was very foggy on Tuesday, so I just started out, just to get them talking, "What was the weather today? Well, what happened Tuesday morning?" and this was . . . a unit we're already past, . . . but it got them to pull that back up to say, you know, what the weather was on Tuesday morning.

I: That's good, yep.

T1: They bring their weather forecast. I have my students bring in a weather forecast after we've done all of this with the weather, to do their weather forecast, you know, we did that a month ago and then, in our Halloween story, the weather forecast came back, there was a gusty day, and the moon was full, and so, our vocabulary came back. I like weather. I like the weather, too.

T3: I love teaching it. I make my students go on the Internet and pick a city in France, and they had to do a four-day forecast for that city, and they had to draw it just like the Channel 9 news, you know, with the little (pantomimes lines) each day, high, low, and then the picture and I made them write the words, too, so you know they learned. I've got one of those still, so I'll bring it to you.

I: That's neat, yeah, if you'll bring that.

T1: I take from the newspaper, our Sunday newspaper has the "Hocus Focus" and you have to find the six differences in the bottom and the top picture and they have to tell me the six differences, and I time them, and they have to come up with all the vocabulary. I do that often, too.

I: That's neat, neat idea. And can they use a dictionary if they don't know how to say it?

T1: If they can do it in the allotted time, or if they can ask their partner. I do that at the beginning of class. I might do that once a week or every two weeks. Just a little something different that . . . they like, so . . .

I: Very good. Anything else? No?

T1: Did I show you my masterpiece, here?

I: Yeah. Today's November the . . . 12th.

T1: Tomorrow's Friday the 13th. The week before Halloween, we were reviewing the *"imparfait,"* the imperfect tense, and we had talked about some adjectives that could describe a frightening experience. And, I like to, as I've said before, do group work. So they were in groups of five, four people to a group, and they had to come up with a story and to narrate in the past. And one person was the secretary, they have to elect a secretary in their group, and then they come up with a story, and I thought this one was good—they have a lot of the *"imparfait"* used correctly, a lot of the *"passé composé"* used correctly, with a little drawing— they signed the bottom—they tell their story and then we look at the way they've used the tenses. So, they've used their grammar point correctly, and it's kind of fun to work together. They learn new words like "pumpkin," I'm sure we had it in French I, but they've just forgotten it. But I thought that was a good activity, they enjoyed it.

I: And this was the first draft, or they have several days to work on it?

T1: Oh, no, this was a class period, less than a class period. Twenty-five minutes. So they got together and did their story.

I: Four in the group, how many students, four?

T1: Yeah, then I have another writing assignment . . . they're responsible for a little story. This is narration again. They were using the *"imparfait"* and *"passé composé."* This takes a little longer. . . . It has to be approved by me before they go on. They can select a story like Madeline, and do their little drawings. I just thought this one came out so well, she did it on her computer.

I: What level?

T1: This is level . . . this was Level Three. They have to turn in a rough draft, and then I have to check the rough draft, and they have to make corrections. They get credit for everything that they do. Their rough draft can be full of mistakes, but then I have their little legend: "Acc" for agreement (accord) and "p" for preposition and "a" for accent, either it's missing or whatever and then they have to make sure they get all their corrections done. I do not help them with their corrections. If they have problems then they have to come in before or after school to get help but then if they submit the final copy full of mistakes, that's when their grade can be lowered. So, this is Madeline, you know, she went to the hospital because she had appendicitis and all her little schoolmates wanted an appendicitis too. They wanted to have an operation also.

T4: That is really cute.

T1: It is cute.

I: Did they make up a story? Or they just . . .

T1: Well, Madeline is . . . a French girl.

I: So, they need to find a famous character.

T1: They need to find a little famous character, probably something that is elementary. Because if it's elementary then you can write about it. If it gets complex, you know, then it's not . . . so they can do a little story like this, or a fairy tale, or someone had done *Hansel and Gretel*.

I: That is neat.

T1: Uh-huh, yeah, she liked Germany and she had gone to Germany and so she did *Hansel and Gretel*. But I thought this one was really, really cute, with no errors at all.

I: They put these together?

T1: Oh, yeah, they put them together.

T2: This is an individual project?

T1: Oh yes, this is an individual project.

T2: Now did you assign topics? Did you just give them a list? Like *Hansel and Gretel*?

T1: Yeah, but I do encourage an activity—that they do something of their own.

T2: She even bound it and everything.

T1: Yeah, oh yeah.

I: How many weeks during the semester . . .

T1: This is a semester project.

I: A semester project.

T1: So they're told about it at the beginning of the semester. They have the entire nine—a nine-week project.

I: So they can revise as many times as they can, as they wish to . . .

T1: And they know where I am if they need some extra help. If I don't see them, and it's still full of mistakes, their grade drops.

I: Because they have the whole semester.

T1: And one more thing I find that's very effective especially for tests. After a chapter. . . . This is a chapter review transparency. This is the culmination of the family chapter. I give this to them as part of their writing component of their exam—their chapter exam and they have to, in a decent paragraph, describe it using as many of the new vocabulary of the chapter as possible.

I: In a paragraph form . . .

T1: In a paragraph form.

I: So they can make up a story?

T1: Make up a story, give the characters' names . . . it was a birthday party, the importance of family in France, that we talked about, that type of thing. And they do a good job at Level One.

I: How, or when, do you start moving from sentence length to paragraph length or longer?

T1: Level One. They write paragraphs in Level One.

I: That's good.

T1: And then . . . they learn how to make a sentence complex, the relative pronoun "that," they can start complex sentences, teach them very elementary conjunctions, joining words like nevertheless, as far as, or thanks to, or . . .

I: When you start with the paragraph-length essay type of writing, do you teach them anything about the writing process? Like prewriting, generating ideas, and then revision?

T1: Yeah. Probably not as much as in an English class. We do some brainstorming. I'd rather do it orally than written . . . we may do some random writing at the beginning of a period. I may put a topic on the board, but . . .

I: But not as much as an English class.

T1: I don't think we have the time to do all that in class, I don't think we have the time.

I: I'd like to go back to grading. How do you grade?

T2: I didn't bring in any samples of what to do as far as writing is concerned. In fact, I wish I had brought what we did in my Spanish III today, because you know, I'm doing the TPRS process, method of teaching. And it's mostly, to begin with, mostly oral working, however with vocabulary, incorporating grammar, and just nouns, some adjectives, whatever, in sentence fragments or just words. They have, you'll learn a sign, or series of signs associated, then we'll practice the signs and make sentences, and eventually we have a story of 100 words long. And in Spanish II what I'll have them do is eventually to draw the story. They listen to me, and I narrate a story, and we have student actors, and they do some hysterical things in class, and of course I do also, but they have listened to me tell the story, I retell the story without actors, with mistakes, and see if they catch on, and they correct me. I'll retell the story with a choice: "Was it the dog, or the cat that was hungry?" and eventually they'll draw the story, tell it to each other two or three times, different people, and I'm walking around . . .

I: And this is oral.

T2: All this was oral. I don't do this every time because there's a time factor, but eventually they'll write it out. Not every single mini-story, but I do like to have them write it out just so they can see the structure involved—they've heard me tell the story over and over again, so the grammar structure, the sentence structure is built in. You'd be amazed at how close to my narration their writing turns out. Today in the Spanish III class we've reached the end of a chapter, so what we've done is taken all the vocabulary from the whole chapter, mini-stories, and they had a series of drawings, they had a grid with 6 blocks. The first block was drawn, the last block was gone. They had to create a story using their vocabulary and they had to draw out their story, and write their story out. Using any vocabulary they wanted to from our chapter and they did a wonderful job. We were working with present perfect tense this time and it did not make it so it would have to be tied to that, but most of them did.

I: That's neat.

T2: I'll try to remember. Some of them read them in class, and they kept them.

I: So you start with that storytelling from Level One?

T2: Yes. I haven't started that because I didn't have any Level Ones this semester, so I started with Level Two. I was nervous about doing it, and then very nervous about doing it in Level Three. So. So far, so good, I've really enjoyed it.

I: Great. Oh, B., we're talking about writing.

T4: Oh . . . I . . . do a lot of group work. I just really feel that it is beneficial for students to learn from one another. And in particular, as we're talking about writing here, the students, when they write something together, if you have a group for example that's got several good students and perhaps several weaker students, the weaker students are going to learn from the better students, and the better students are going to learn more by helping the weaker students. I just find it really helps, plus it's very creative, and so forth, so there's lots of things you can do with that. . . . I just photocopied some examples of some things in Spanish II, we had done some room descriptions because we were working on descriptions, and these were some group things that they did, and obviously their rooms weren't the same so they had to choose a person in the group and choose which room to describe and do that. So there's some examples of that.

I: And they do that in one period, two?

T4: They do that in ten minutes. You can't give them long to do something like that, because it was a pretty simple assignment.

I: And how often do you give this type of assignment?

T4: Every couple of weeks or so. And sometimes we do it individual and sometimes we do it in groups. So they're getting, having to do it themselves, and getting to do it in groups, and learning from one another in that way. Also, in Level Three, the textbook that we are using has a workbook that comes with it and it has a wonderful section in it called "*Escribamos*," "Let's Write," and I just started out, and I photocopied some of this for you, but this is scattered over several chapters, because each chapter has a section called "*Escribamos*," but it starts out with the construction of a sentence, it goes very basic, even though it's Level Three, just to touch back with them and say, "Let's identify subject-verb complement, and just make sure we know what we're doing." And then you start adding in additional words, you've got "*Palabras Adicionales*" so you've got a time factor, then you start adding in adjectives, so it shows you a sentence that's too vague, and what's more precise, then it gives them adverbs, how you can add in adverbs, oh, then it starts the development of an idea, how you start with an idea then you add an argument to it, then it gives them idea, argument, and example, then it gives them the organization of a paragraph, you see, and how you can put a paragraph together, then it tells them you need an introductory sentence, "One or more ideas or arguments, one or more examples and then concluding statement," and then of course all along they're doing practice with each of these things. It is a great workbook as far as writing, then how to do connecting words, how to connect your paragraphs, how to connect your sentences, more of those and how to do summaries. And with the summaries, it gives them ideas, they actually get examples of things that have been summarized, then they have to do some summaries themselves.

I: How do you use this in the classroom?

T4: Well, . . . the process of doing that, and then we just do a lot of these things, for example, I was out last week for the FLANC conference, and one of the things I had them do is read a selection of information, cultural information, actually, that they needed for an upcoming test and to do a summary of it, because we had already done how to do a summary of it, we had been through all that process. They did this as groups, this was a group thing, they had to read a selection, close their books and then do a summary. But they were doing it in groups, so even though they were closing their books, they were . . .

I: Sharing . . .

T4: Because if you'd had them leave their books open, they'd just copy. But, they closed their books, but everybody remembers something different. And so here are some examples of some summaries that they did with that. And then the other thing that I wanted to share as far as writing is . . . but in Spanish III, at the end of the year we do a review of preterit and imperfect. And I have them do a project, and it's about a three-week-long project, we go through a process, and they do fairy tales, and so I think it's similar, I didn't hear what you were saying, but I think it's similar to what you do, and they can take an already-existing fairy tale and just narrate it, or they can make their own, or they can take one that already exists and change it in some way. . . . For example they can take the *Three Little Pigs* and make the pigs the bad guys and make the wolf the good guy or they can change it any way they want to and then they have to put it together in a book form.

I: That is neat.

T4: Um, this of course is *The Lion King*, and that is the way I grade that, so when we get to grading, I'll show you that, so anyway . . .

I: So this is group work? Or individual?

T4: This is individual. This is individual. So they have to narrate it and they have to illustrate it, and illustrating can be doing their own illustrations, or just cutting, just doing cut-outs, which a lot of them do cut-outs, and I just ran over them and picked some up, I wish I had brought one that was illustrated, but I don't think I did. This is *Rapunzel* . . . and she did just a super job on this. This is really just the way she did this . . . but of course the idea is just the uses of the past tenses and that they get that right. . . .

I: And you said this was a three-week project?

T4: The process . . . we have a process that we do with this. I have them do a rough draft, before we even start on this part, and they turn their rough draft in and I have a grading rubric that I use, a . . . grading code that I use, and basically I circle the mistakes and tell them what type of mistake it is, I don't correct it for them. Then they get their rough draft back and then they have to start putting it together—That's when they do this part—this is *Blanca Nieves*, *Snow White*, and again they can put it together however they want, this is the *Three Little Pigs*, . . . typed up with illustrations, however they want to do that, and some of them do their own illustrations and I just grabbed a few off the top and didn't grab one that had their own illustrations. This, however, has . . . the way she did hers was she did it with pop-ups.

I: Can I see this? Let me zoom that.

T4: There's a little invitation to the ball that pops up, and then . . . let's see how this one works, you just pull it, there's the other part of that . . .

I: Opens up . . .

T4: Yeah, opens up and then, she has . . . them dancing across the floor, so she did that as a pop-up, pull-out, whatever you want to call it . . . then of course it's all narrated in Spanish. This is about a three-week project, as I've said . . . I make the assignment and they have to do their rough draft. They have approximately a week to do their rough draft and I get that back to them in about a week, and they have a week to complete it. And this is of course after we've done a review of preterit and imperfect—it is review at the beginning of Spanish III, because we've done a fairly thorough study of it towards the end of Spanish II, so pretty quick review and then we just kind of pull it all together by doing the stories.

I: And you do that at Level Three, right?

T4: This is at the beginning, the very beginning of Level Three, as a review. But it's a nice uniting project. I've done it for a number of years and have some beautiful, beautiful books that they've put together for me and I don't give them back—so I have lots of them!

I: Ah, that's neat.

T4: They supply all their own materials. They supply everything. However they want to do it. They will laminate—a lot of them do laminate, which makes a very nice book, it really is nicely put together, and one thing I do with this . . . if there are mistakes in here, and hopefully they've eliminated a lot of them, though certainly not all of them, I don't do any corrections in this . . . and this is one of the rough drafts by the way, so you can kind of see what that looks like, so they just turn the rough draft in on regular notebook paper . . . anything that's wrong? Just circle it, the "D" stands for "deletreo" and that's spelling, and then they get this back in this way and what I end up doing . . . we don't want to talk about correction yet . . .

I: No, not yet, not yet. Good, that's great; M. wants to see them.

T4: Sure, sure.

T3: I wonder if they could go to Barnes and Noble and buy an inexpensive children's book and cut it up?

T1: Go to Target and get them. They could do that, yeah.

T4: That's what a lot of them do. They buy the book and cut it up—that's how they got those kinds of illustrations. And that's what I tell them—that you don't have to be able to draw to do a nice job or something like this.

T3: Yeah, I tell them I can't draw, either.

T4: The idea is to put something neat together and of course to do it well.

I: Yeah, neat. How interested are you—you're doing similar things?

T1: Yeah, I do the rough draft, and then we . . .

I: Oh, B.? . . .

T2: Mr. B. who got here late is puzzled but he'll show you what he's got. And he'll just show it to you! He might not be very coherent with his comments, but . . .

I: We'll edit the tape.

T2: OK, I . . . in writing, I like to do dictation . . . sometimes I just give them a dictation totally where they're providing everything—all the information—and then other times I will give them something like that (shows paper) where I have simply given them some basic sentences and left out the words. This came from the French III textbook, in Chapter 3, and it's packed full of vocabulary, except a lot of the vocabulary is missing. They had to have studied vocabulary that we'd gone over and do dictations . . . and yet I don't depend on dictations as a primary learning tool but I like to use dictations as a means of—I call it my counteraction to human nature. And I've asked the student, sometimes I say, "What is human nature? Is human nature to go home and study this nightly? Nope." I say even we teachers, we have to force ourselves to do something sometimes . . . it forces them to have to look at the vocabulary and I figure the more I can get them looking at it, the more retention there's going to be.

I: And you tell them in advance, that there will be a dictation, or it's like a test?

T2: Most of the time I tell them in advance . . . what areas that they need to be familiar with. Sometimes I give them the dictation in one form, like this, and the very next day I will give them something with the same sentences but sometimes additional words have been left out or rearranged.

I: Could I have a copy of that?

T2: Sure. I like to write stories, as I've said before, and this is not a really good writing activity, but I guess it serves as a foundation for them writing on their own, and this is a story about two people going to a café, and I just made it up, trying to include as much vocabulary and some of the things they have to do on the Chapter 5 test is to write a paragraph on their own, wherein they have two fictitious characters going to a café from start to finish and they have to tell me in order the things that they do, as long as it makes sense. I don't want them getting the food before they order it, or something like that; I like to do the transparencies like this, wherein I create a story . . .

I: Oh, but before you get into that, tell me more about the previous one. So you use that as a model to teach—to show them how you did it, right?

T2: Yes, just as a model, and sometimes we'll do one together on the board, I like to take big—those huge sheets of paper, like those elementary teachers use—and put it on the board with clips, and sometimes we'll write one together where all I am is the scribe, and they're the energy and they're telling me, and I'm just composing it so everybody can see it. And sometimes I'll use one of your tricks (points to SB) . . . and if say the verb conjugation comes out wrong, I'll kind of go . . . "Very good, J'ai bien compris ce que tu as dit," I understand what you said, BUT . . . and then somebody in the room will self-correct it, and then I'll go, "Beautiful," and then in the end, for positive feedback, you thank the person who gave the correction and then you thank the person who gave the idea. Because the person who's got the idea, you can't stifle their—they provided the energy, even though they conjugated the verb wrong.

I: Yeah, yeah.

T2: So you thank both of them and you write that sentence to the story and then you move on.

I: That's good, and also you're giving the idea that writing is not only grammar, but content . . .

T2: Right. I tell them on tests, they always ask me, on the subjective part, how long does it have to be?

T4: I know.

T2: How long does it have to be? And I usually tell them, it's like eating my aunt's carrot cake. I'd rather have one slice of her carrot cake than a whole stale pound cake. I'd rather have five awesome sentences than eight bunch-of-junk that's poorly written and used nothing new from the chapter. In the past, I have had students to do a brochure . . . I said, "Your job is, you work for the NC Department of Tourism in Raleigh and your assignment is . . . the state of NC is interested in attracting tourists from France to come to this part of the country, and you've got to come up with something that would cause French-speaking people to want to come here." And so they've come up with an idea and they do their little thing, "Le Vacation Varietyland"—a little *"franglais"*—and then they just write, and then fill it with pictures and they have to tell me about the different things that can be done, and then see the back?

I: And this is an individual project?

T2: Individual. That was in Level Three, from about three or four years ago. And so they would put the lighthouses up and say, "Welcome to North Carolina. The state is divided into three regions," and then he talks about the regions and puts little captions. And of course he has some grammar errors, but for the most part is pretty good. And this they did not have to do a rough draft for, so this could be perfected with the rough draft.

T1: Make them do a rough draft so you can save the final copy.

T2: That's right, make them do a rough draft so that you can get those mistakes out of there.

I: And that's another point that I want to emphasize, that writing is a process, that they can make it better, and better, and better, all the time.

T2: Oh yes, definitely.

I: So, that's a good point that you mentioned because at the beginning you didn't realize . . .

T2: True.

I: As a new teacher, tell me your story, B.

T2: Well, once upon a time . . . I was just interested in a project and I wasn't aware of the process . . .

T1: Process to get there . . .

T2: . . . So then I said, then you go home and say, "Man, we've gone over that verb five thousand times, and you still don't have it." And then you find out that it would be much better to take them through the process. And then let them see, give them feedback and go through . . . all the stages. And then you learn as you go, you really do, just like learning to teach is a process. Just like writing is a process.

I: Absolutely. That's an important point.

T2: But I enjoyed doing that.

I: But I interrupted you when you were showing the transparency . . .

T2: Oh, that's fine. The transparency is nothing more than a vocabulary check. (To T1) And you might want a copy, because you're starting Chapter 5, right?

T1: We've started Chapter 5, yeah.

T2: This is just a follow-up of Chapter 4, and it just gets to a place where they have to come up with—they have to pick the verb—so it's more vocabulary than it is writing. But then again it gives them an idea to see written French. If you want to incorporate technology, go on to the Internet and find a website for weather and tell your students they've got to choose a French-speaking city of the world and they've got to compose it in their own words, the weather conditions. And this girl did an outstanding job. This was last year and she did it for Quebec City. . . . And she has total the weather, what it's going to be, she has temperatures converted to Celsius and she's a *South Park* fan, evidently (points to "Kenny" drawing a picture). She did an excellent job. That's one of the best ones I've ever had. And then, this person, we didn't just do France, we did some of France's possessions in the South Pacific Ocean (project is of Leon, New Caldonia). And, you see how much hotter it is there. And, she did a good job, I think. Then we went to France and did Lyon. And there is *vendredi, samedi, dimanche, lundi,* and they did just the weather. And this was just a use of the Internet-type project which caused them to have to write something. One of my favorite writing activities ever was the year that I made them do a project on their house. And Chapter 7 I think it is of the French II textbook, is real big on the house and I am under block scheduling, so I'm putting two chapters together. So, like, when I teach Chapter 4, I also give most of the vocabulary of Chapter 9 as well. It's just loaded with vocabulary. But this girl, they had to draw their house, or their dream house, and then they had to draw a blueprint to it, and describe it underneath and again, this should be a process to make it the best that it can possibly be. So they're learning the rooms of the house and then the person has to draw the house and use as much vocabulary, and describe it in the best way, and I thought she did an outstanding job. She's artistic as well as skilled in French. You see only a few errors, and like I said, you can eliminate having to do this by carrying them through the process.

T4: What did you do, B., with people who can't draw?

T2: Just draw the best they can. And if they want to bring in pictures, that's fine.

T1: Cut-outs?

T2: Cut-outs, sure. Any way you illustrate it is fine with me. But, that's one of the best pictures I've ever seen.

T4: That is nice.

T2: But, she did a good job, too. And also I just had another example of some of the same thing. Where they drew a kitchen and then, "*Ma cuisine est très grande pour une cuisine. Je vais . . .*" I see, and then she tells what she sees . . . "I see a faucet, a dishwasher," and on and on and then she made a classic "*de le*" error. But, she did a good job. I was proud of them. I thought they did a—it caused them to think.

I: And how many weeks do you spend on that?

T2: We usually spend, if I give this assignment on Monday, we're usually ready to turn it in on Friday or the next week, so not too long.

I: One, one more question: Do you do the work in class? Or . . .

T2: Some, and some at home and sometimes I do monitoring in class . . . and if you're going to do process writing, I would suggest that you do a lot definitely in class for that, because you've got all the ingredients there for correction. And I'll tell you what I think is good, too, is let them pass their work to a trusted neighbor. Not to someone who's lagging behind, for the purpose of just stealing ideas, but let someone else give some feedback on it—the peer could teach—see if the peer, like, "Sarah, are you able to understand what Beth is trying to say?" And, I think that's really good. The months of the year thing was really good. They had you do the table of contents and then do some writing. And again, process would have eliminated the errors, but anyway, they did the simplest of drawings, and then they had to write, and just tell me things that were going on in that month. They had to describe the weather in that month, because when I teach Chapter 4, months, I also teach weather and things they like to do in that month. She did a good job. And, I don't know why, this doesn't look "high-schoolish," but if you can get them to draw, some of them love to do it so much, the energy for this is coming off the excitement of doing this, and that's my opinion.

T2: True, true. Of course this one she got kind of simple on, but just the idea of being able to . . .

I: Motivating them . . .

T2: Yeah, it motivates them. Yeah, they do a good job. (Reading from December:) *"J'aime beaucoup le mois décembre parce que mon aniversaire est le deux. Si je m'achetais des cadeaux . . . "*

T2: And I pack them full of vocabulary and I try to tell them . . . I also think in writing, of course they've got to do it because English is their language and we've talked about that in these sessions before, but I tell them sometimes, "Try not to think in English," because they'll come up to you, and you'll be trying to get them to write something about November, and they'll say, "Mr. G., how do you say 'the leaf slowly floated and caressed the leaves as it fell'?" And I'll go, "I couldn't even say that in French." I mean, and then I said, "Get real," and so I said, and so you've got to tell them, "Stop and think, how long have you been studying French? Three months, right?" And so . . .

T1: Stick with what you know.

T2: Stick with what you know. Communicate.

T4: They won't do that. They want to . . .

T2: I know. The last thing I'll show you probably has nothing to do with writing, but I brought it, so I'll show it. This is my classic concentration game, and it reviews numbers. And you put them on the board with a clip—and they have magnetic clips you can buy at K-Mart—you just take a piece of construction paper and you put a number on one side, and some phrase on the other side. And you mix them up so they're all over the board, and my board's magnetic and so they call out the number—*vingt-et-un*, and you turn—I go up and turn—that one around and then they have to call another number. Which, then you turn that one around and then if you were to turn around, say, that number (Card says "*un examen*"—a test) then you would say, "Do those make sense together? No, it doesn't make a sentence together." So they would have to remember where "*nous habitons*" was and then if suddenly they were to say (looks through numbers) that one will work—"*rue Saint-Dominique*," we live on St. Dominique Street. So, that would be a match and those stay through and really if it's a Friday, you go to the Trademart and buy a bag of Tootsie Rolls and toss one to each person who makes a match.

T4: Same game—whenever they play the game it's the same phrases?

T1: They have to memorize the pairs.

T2: Right, well, you only play it one time per class—then that's it, but if you're like one student, whose name I won't call because you're taping this, he wrote down the number combinations and passed them out at lunch.

T1: Oh my goodness!

I: But imagine all the energy spent on that.

T2: I'll tell you, but that was all right. Oh, brother. But he only gave it out to like one person.

I: That is something. But the distribution of a grade or Tootsie Roll perk. OK, great, great ideas. Two questions for you: How do you decide on a topic? What do you have in mind when you think about, "OK, I want them to write about a story? Or about a room?" Why do you choose the topic that you choose?

T1: With the Level One and Two, you really just have to stick with the chapter, with the vocabulary you just learned. If it's Chapter 4 Level One, on the family, it has to be using that vocabulary.

I: OK.

T1: Don't you agree?

T4: I agree. It has to be related with what you're doing in the book, what you're doing in class in some way. Otherwise you're just doing something random and it's not going to mean anything.

I: So there's really only one ingredient.

T4: Authentic, authentic! There we go. It's got to be authentic. I think that in your upper levels it can also be seasonal. And what I mean by seasonal is, whatever holiday happens to be taking place at that particular time, Christmas, anything like that, but it would have to be in Levels, say, Three and Four, possibly. Because you're kind of stuck in the first two levels.

I: Oh, so related to the material, seasonal, authentic, what do you think when you sit down and say, "OK, I'm going to make them write about this." Why and why not, no, I don't like this, how do you choose?

T4: What they, you want to choose something that they're going to enjoy writing about. For Level One and Level Two, so if you have several possible topics in the chapter, depending on the vocabulary you're working on, you know, for example, that writing we did about their rooms—they're going to enjoy writing about their own rooms more than they would describing the cafeteria and the school, or something that's not personal to them, so you want to pick something they would enjoy writing about among the things that you have in the vocabulary or within that structure you're working on.

I: OK.

T1: And after you've done it several times, it's whatever has worked best for you: One year you may select a topic that really wasn't successful so you change it the following year, that type of thing, so from experience you get to feel which topics are better for them.

I: Any other ideas? No? How detailed are you when giving directions for the topic?

T4: I think you have to be relatively detailed in what you want, you need to tell them, you know, "You must include the vocabulary we've been working on; you must get the particular structure or form you've been working on." They must include that, I also always like to tell them to be creative but not so creative, like B. was saying, that they want to say impossible things, but they need to stick within structures, and vocabulary, and word, and they can always go over and use the dictionaries, but there are problems with that also. . . . But particularly the lower the level, the more structured it is, really the better the writing's going to be. But if you just say, "Write about your room," you're just going to have too much of a hodgepodge of possibilities. Something else I've found that you also need to include is a minimum number of words to use, otherwise you'll have, like if they're supposed to write a paragraph on their room, and sometimes I don't always limit it to their own room, because I know that some of these kids come from situations where it may not be anything they want to talk about, so, say, an imaginary room they would love to have . . .

T3: I do the same thing.

T4: So I know that if I put that in there, I know it won't be such a limited subject, so I say, "You need to have about 50 words or so," because if not, sometimes you'll just get two sentences. They may be great sentences, but I want them to learn how to describe and I feel like lots of times, depending on what the subject is, you need to, particularly with the lower levels, let them know you need to have a certain number of words in there.

T1: And the words, and the expressions you want them to use.

T4: See, in storytelling what I do also is we'll take vocabulary that we just worked on, say, for a mini-story, and they're just words, or phrases, and they're to create a totally new story, have those phrases in there, or those words, or those grammar structures. And then they do all that also, and that's been an interesting production.

I: Great, about writing, how do you grade writing? You have some rubrics and some . . . ?

T4: For my project, the booklets that we do, that are like this and I have this sheet that I use, which is based on points—20 points for the rough draft, and that 20 points is based on: is it turned in on time, and how many errors were in the rough draft, and that keeps them from turning in a rough draft, just throwing something together just to get it in on time, so they are held responsible for the number of errors in the rough draft. And you have to be relatively specific with that, so I will actually count the number of errors there, in that rough draft, and say for example, of that 20 points, I might knock off one point for every 10 errors, or something along that line, so this person for example got 16 out of 20 points for their rough draft, then 20 points for originality, and that includes illustrations, neatness, creativity, and then basically she did an excellent job. And this was the one who did the pop-ups, so I actually gave her more than 20 points on that, because she did such a great job on that and this section, which is really half of the grade is 50 points, and that's the actual grammar, which is really what we were working on, the preterit and the imperfect, and so they still have mistakes after the rough draft and after correction, and she actually had quite a few and instead of correcting them here (places hand on student's book) I write them on here (grading sheet) on this sheet, and then they get this sheet. And I'll write what the actual correction was, and the number of mistakes is going to be quite a bit less than the rough draft, because they've had the advantage of knowing what the mistake was, and still did not correct it, so with this one, for every two mistakes, it's one point off of that 50. And then the fourth category is really a catch-all 10 points for the cover, what they do with the cover, just kind of overall—the general impression of that—and that equals 100 points, and that's just one, that's just how I do that project.

I: And you grade the drafts mainly [for] the grammar?

T4: The drafts, yeah, because the originality and ideas are taken into account in a different section. So the rough draft is totally whether or not it's on time and how many mistakes.

T1: I do the same thing when we do a project, it's 100 points, and of course the bulk of it is their writing, which is the purpose, but they do get some points for creativity, for the final product and for the rough draft. I don't count each mistake, if they—and they're going to—make the same mistakes over and over again. I use my little legend and what I would prefer is that they do is correct correctly—to go back and think about their errors—that's the whole purpose, so if they've done a good job, if they've told their story, if they're anywhere between the four and five page range, I know they've spent some time on it, they'll probably get the bulk of the 20 for their rough draft. But what really counts is whether they've made their corrections, that's the purpose, really, of mastering the difference between the imperfect and the past tense. But, in class, for an in-class writing assignment, it depends on the assignment, it depends on the topic, it depends on what we've covered, a paragraph of five sentences might be five points apiece, 25 points, depending on. . . . It really depends. The way I grade really depends on the assignment.

T4: It really does.

T1: And I find that grading writing that, you young teachers out there, that you take a writing workshop, and you learn from your colleagues, and you ask questions, "How do you grade? How do you grade?" and get different ideas for grading writing because it's probably the hardest to grade, of everything to grade. It's so subjective and yet you have to be objective—you have to have that number grade on the paper, and it's hard, it's very difficult.

T4: And starting out, you know, sometimes I think it's helpful to have someone else look at the same paper and maybe not even let them see what you put on it—cover the grade up somehow if you can—and say, "What grade would you have given this?" and get some cross-reference that way.

T1: I wanted to say something about—a student automatically looks at his neighbor's paper, "Well, what did YOU make?" or, "What did she give you?" Especially if he's really not satisfied with the grade, to always, always tell them, "This is a contract between you and me, don't share with your neighbor, always come to me and we'll talk about it and we'll talk about why did you get a 26 out of 30 instead of a 30 out of 30," to be able to discuss with the student how you came up with that grade. And that might be very difficult, too. So always be ready to evaluate verbally how you came up with that. I think that's just as important as giving the grade.

T4: I just wanted to add one thing. This semester with my Level Twos when they've been writing, I haven't really assigned what I would call "formal" writing assignments a lot. They'll turn in, for example, the stories that they've written, we have quizzes on stories where they have to give specific answers to specific questions about the story—when it's something like that, what I'm giving is a participation grade, more than anything—make sure they do it, and I don't necessarily grade it because they're so excited about being able to write and to speak it that I really don't feel like they would know enough to make corrections. But I do in Level Three make corrections on the things they turn in, the stories they read. Today I walked around and read them all, and the corrections that were necessary and I made them myself because we didn't have time today to do a legend-type thing but now I'm planning, it's kind of funny because you have both the fairy tales, because a project I'm going to assign for my Threes in the last two or three weeks of school is going to be to create a fairy tale and I got that idea from somewhere else, but I loved seeing yours. But for that, I would have a rubric similar to what you've got. I've had several ideas from the "FL Teach" list, and so then we'll go through the process, because that a finished product they could revise on their own. But, like I said in the first couple of levels I really do that much correcting. Just as long as they're producing, and I can pretty much understand what they're saying, I'm not going to stifle that. So, then when they get more advanced they'll need to know that.

I: Great. B.—grading.

T3: You have to, you've got to be careful, and you've got to know how you're going to approach it before you approach it and you've got to know what you want, and you've got to make sure they know what you want.

T4: Rubrics are invaluable. They eliminate any questions. You have it in black and white. They can't say, "Well, you didn't say . . ."

I: You mentioned two things, one is *you* know what you want them to do, and the other is *they* know what you want them to do.

T3: Right. If you're not on the same page then you're not gonna get what you want.

I: So how do you do that?

T3: Communicate really well.

I: And the other point that you raised is, I always tell my prospective teachers that they should never think that the students will understand things that they hadn't said.

T2: They can't read your mind.

T3: Repetition. It's amazing how many things you also can say one time that will not be retained by the students, and you think, "I said it. That's it. Why didn't you understand?" Well, you have to repeat it, and sometimes you have to say it in different ways. Not just repeat it.

T1: And if they know what to expect, if it's on paper in black and white, it teaches them a sense of responsibility. "I know I've got to do it this way and this way and this way."

T3: I love to make a student stand up and select somebody . . . who would be very uncomfortable so you might not call on them to do this, so this definitely wouldn't be a requirement for the class—but have one student stand up and tell everybody: "What's the assignment? What do we have to do? And that person restates—it's amazing how they listen to their own peers, because some of them are just waiting for that person to make a mistake so they can go, 'No, he didn't say that!' " And then, so they're totally focused on that student.

T4: And if you use rubrics, which are wonderful to use, and I agree with you, C., if the student has the rubric ahead of time, you know, before they start the project, then they know what you're looking for, they know how they'll be graded, and there shouldn't be any question.

I: Absolutely. Do you have any examples of rubrics you have used?

T4: Not here with me.

T1: I think I have one in my office.

T4: I just white the name out.

I: It really brings more life to that sheet that you use to grade.

T3: I think it would bring more life to your classes at ECU.

I: Yes, yes, it's for my students.

T3: Because it would be something *real*.

T1: This was a Level One project we did last spring on Paris. I had research and information, presentation of material, illustrations and bibliography, and if you get a 3, your monument was considered like the Taj Mahal, if you get a 2, it was just the Chambord, if you had a 3 it was the Biltmore. And they have their criteria. This was a very elementary rubric but it worked for this particular project.

T1: And then they know if they make a 12, an 11 or 12, that they have an A, and that's an A, that's anywhere from a 93 to a 100—and I control that.

I: And this is given beforehand?

T1: Oh, yeah, they know, they get this with the project. They know when they get a major project they'll have a rubric for it.

T3: Do you do . . . oh I see, so if someone made a 9, they get 9 points, is that what you're saying?

T1: From this, yes.

T3: From that, yeah. IF someone got a 9, and this person got 10, do you differentiate here?

T1: Oh, yes. I differentiate. I have the right—they may make a 9, but I have the right to decide in that range what it is. One 9 might be better than another 9, that kind of thing.

T3: Yeah. But they're guaranteed at least an 80, right?

T1: Yeah. It's pretty simple.

I: Great. Any other comments on how you grade writing?

SESSION #4

I: It's December 10th, and we're going to talk about motivation, class participation, and discipline. So, we welcome your insights and ideas. Who wants to start?

T4: I'll start. I'm going to talk about my oral participation sheet, because I really think this covers all three of the areas that you're talking about: it's motivation, there's a grade tied to it; it also in a sense deals with discipline, they can't speak English without permission or they get an "F" on this sheet, and therefore in many ways that really helps with discipline; and of course it involves class participation. But basically, what I have is this sheet covers an entire semester, and I'll let you have a copy of the sheet. Each of the little blocks represents a day in the semester, so I have across the top, Monday through Friday.

I: So they do one a week.

T4: Well, one line represents a week. This is for the whole semester. This will cover one whole semester. They get this sheet every day at the be-ginning of class, and I take it up every day at the end of class. So this line, one line then is a week. This is a nine-week period and this is a nine-week period, so this is one semester. And so each day—this is a self-evaluation tool—the students evaluate themselves according to the rubric that I have on the back of the paper so every day they will put in a grade of "A," "B," "C," "D," or "F" as I take them back up each day, I check them immediately so I don't forget what they've done in class, and if I disagree with the grade, I will change it. So they do eval-uate themselves, but they know that I'm going to be looking at it, and if they have not evaluated themselves correctly, then I will change the grade. At the end of the week, I total up their points, an "A" is 4 points, a "B" is 3, a "C" is 2, a "D" is one, zero for an "F." If, for example, on a given week they had five fours, that would be 20 points. Then at the end of the marking period I total up all the points, put it on a scale, and give them a grade on that, which counts as a major test.

I: So this is a major test.

T4: So it will end up counting as much as a major test counts. Now, here's the motivation and discipline, which is the rubric itself: They earn an "F" if they speak any English without permission or if they don't ever speak a word of Spanish during class. So, that's two reasons for getting an "F." They also get an "F" if they have not completed their homework, because if they have not completed homework, they really can't participate in what we're doing every day, so, it's motivating to do homework, because they're getting a grade here every day; and motivating to participate, because it's basically a participation, it's speaking and listening, it's oral and aural. And so what they have to do is they start with a "D" and can work up to an "A," it doesn't work the other way around. In other words, they cannot look at the "A" requirements and just do that, if they haven't done the "D," "C," and "B" requirements, so they start at the bottom, really, and work up, is what they do. So for example, for a "D," they can just come and sit in class, they've completed their homework, and some time during class they've spoken some Spanish, to get a "D" for the day.

I: That's good.

T4: For a "C," they have to have done everything that "D" says, plus cooperate and participate with their groups, and we're doing group work almost every day. . . . So they can come in class, work with their groups, which means they've spoken some Spanish during the day, not speaking any English, they've done their homework and they can make a "C." OK? For a "B," they have to do all of that, plus, they have to have their hand in the air and they have to be participating. Not just my calling on them, but their hand has got to be in the air. It's got to be voluntary. So, that is a motivater for them to participate. It's a motivater for them to speak Spanish, it's a motivater for them to have their homework, because it's tied here to what we're doing. And it does have to be voluntary. And then for the grade of "A," they have to have done all three, they have to have done all those things plus, they have to give me some language they have created themselves. And that has to be documented on a little sticky note: I keep little sticky notes up on my table all the time. You'll see them come in they'll go grab one and pick it up, and the reason is that just in case I don't look over these papers immediately—I try to do that, but you know things happen and sometimes you don't—if I don't get to this, to first period's papers 'till the end of the day, I may not remember what John said during first period, so putting that little sentence on that sticky note documents for me that they have indeed given me an original sentence—that they created some language. It also says to them, "Don't you put down an 'A' on that paper unless you have that little sticky note on there that says what you have said in class." And they can't just write it down. There has to have been some time that they have said it in class. And as we've talked about before, there are plenty of times at the beginning of class that I give them time to talk and there's their opportunity for an original sentence. But there are days when you have just got to get through your material, there's a test the next day, you've already assigned and you've got to get through it so you may not have that five minutes at the beginning of class, they're still held responsible. They will have to find a way some-time during class to ask me a question, to come up with something that is pertinent to what we're doing. But where they have created language and not just regurgitated something back to me from a homework as-signment, or from somewhere. So they have to have created something. Now, for, let me say this: for someone who's just starting out in teaching, this can be a little overwhelming keeping up with all this, because it really does require looking at these things immediately, you cannot let it go a day. Or you would not remember who had their hand in the air, of course you have their sentence documented, but as far as remember-ing, so you have got to do it then or you won't remember it, so then, it becomes an invalid tool. But for me, it works really well, I'm used to doing it, but it's still a lot of work, but . . . I find that it really motivates the students to participate in class. And, because you know when you've been in my class, or when observers have been in my class, that they've got their hands in the air, because they want that, at least that "B."

I: How do the students react? Do they like it, or they complain? Or . . .

T4: They don't complain. They really don't, they like it. I think it gives them . . . for students who maybe don't do well at, because it's commu-nicative, if maybe you have a student who just doesn't test well, who doesn't do well on tests, he can count on this being a good grade if he'll just do it.

I: Absolutely.

T4: And since that counts as a major test, it's something that can really help the grade, but it also really motivates them, and as I say, it's a good discipline tool, too, since they can't speak English without permission, unless they make an "F," how are they going to misbehave in Spanish? You know? It keeps them . . . you know, if they're talking to one another, when they're not supposed to be talking or whatever, it better be in Spanish.

I: That's right.

T4: Or they earn that "F" for the day. And unless they've asked me permission, they can ask me permission if they really can't express themselves. But then I encourage them to try to say what they can, and then ask, "¿Cómo se dice?" and try to fit that into their sentence . . . but it really helps them . . . and encourages them to create language. So I really find it's a wonderful motivator, and a discipline tool all at the same time.

I: Do they understand it easily or do you have to go over it and . . . take a day as an example?

T4: I spend an entire day at the beginning of the year explaining it to them, and going over lots of different scenarios and stuff, and then the first week they evaluate themselves and I check them very, very closely so that they know if they put down "B" and I mark it down to a "C," I'll write them a little note and say, "You did not raise your hand voluntarily today. I called on you but you did not volunteer," you know.

I: You have to be very disciplined also, in following . . .

T4: You have to be very disciplined and consistent, but once they get the hang of it, they very rarely give themselves an incorrect grade, once they get the hang of it. Sometimes I have to mark them down, sometimes they won't have their homework and they'll go ahead and participate and do everything, I'll walk around the room and check homework as we're going over it, and then I just have to remember who didn't have it, and that sort of thing and if they didn't have their homework they may but a "B" down for the day, and I'll mark it through and put an "F," and write above it "tarea" (homework). So they know why it's been changed. But, I find, it works very well for me, and as I say, it is a lot of work for the teacher, in just being consistent enough, and following through and keeping up with it and if you don't do that, then it's not a good tool; it's a great tool if you discipline yourself enough to do it.

I: Yeah. The students who have come here to observe you, they all love it. It's excellent. I think you're really keeping them on track.

T2: I'd like to have a copy of that, too, because of the structure of the TPRS, so much of the anticipation is delayed, and you don't, the thinking is that you don't want to rush anybody into speaking, necessarily. One of the things that I do is I have a log that I keep. I have a list of the students' names, and then, two columns in which we have a breakdown of grades by five points. Opposite from S., they start off with a bank of 100 points, for their participation, OK, and you've got their name and you've got a column with 100, 05, 09, 80 and so on. And there's another column and this is my "págame" ("pay me") and there are not that many requirements, which I think I will change, this has been my first semester with it, so . . . I'll be adapting it, but the very few requirements that I have for getting *"págame"* in class is, when I say you only speak in Spanish that you only speak in Spanish, similar to what you do, and then they have to ask permission to speak in English. Unfortunately, I haven't been that strict with it—it's been difficult for me to get in that mode of thinking. I've already got plans on how to do that with Spanish I, kids who've never had that before in another type of system. . . . Anyway, the second requirement is to participate at least in the sign language. If they don't speak it's okay, but they must at least be doing the signs. I added a 3rd, "off-task behavior," if . . . a TPRS class is busier, and a bit more talkative than a very structured classroom and so if you're kidding around with your neighbor when you're not supposed to be, but it's in Spanish, it's not so bad, but when you're talking across the room about yesterday's football game, that is a disruption to the class, so I include that in my list of *"págame."* All right, so I have this inside a clear—inside one of those clear plastic slips and I just have it with me, and I just say, "So and so, *págame."* Now, the plus side to this is there's another column where they can make up *"págame."* Some systems do different things, like for example if you've been absent, that's going to take away a five-point. It'll earn you one, because you can't make an absence up, and you can't make the participation for that day up. But there might be another way you can do it, if you've done your work for that day or whatever. But on the "payback" what I have them do, they get four "free" paybacks, make me a card, it can't be bought, it can't be done in class, they can only give me two a week, but they have to say things like, "You are the best Spanish teacher in the world! I love you so very much! I mean this from the bottom of my heart!" But they have to make the effort, and it has to be a personally made effort. After that, and I haven't had anyone go beyond making three or four, and I haven't given that much, that many *"págames"* out, then they start in having to do a composition in Spanish, using the storytelling techniques we've been using in class, but we haven't had anyone go that far yet, so I'm not sure how that would turn out. But that also takes care of the discipline, like you said, it's all integrated into the same thing. They're motivated to want to participate, because it doesn't count as a test grade, but their participation at the end of the six weeks is worth 25 percent, or a quarter of the six weeks' grade . . . and wherever they end up, say they earn four *"págames,"* but they give two back, then they have a 90 for their participation grade for that six weeks. And it works fairly well.

I: And do they do self-evaluate, or do you evaluate them?

T2: I evaluate them. Now, it's sometimes negotiable, depending . . . Sometimes it's difficult to say who started what. Some children are masters at setting others up, to take the fall for them, and so, that's not occurred very often, where we had to sit down and really talk about what happened . . . that's just what I do—just keep that sheet with me at all times and with an erasable pen, what I do at the end of the six weeks is wipe that sheet clean and start all over again.

I: Good idea. Do you mind bringing it in next time?

T2: I will bring it in . . . I'm going to make more requirements. And I have to be stricter about the language part, the speaking part. What's happened is just about all these students had me before when I was not trying to focus so much on target language and so it was easy for me to fall off the very demanding tone. But when I start with my Spanish Is next semester, I hope to discipline myself even better, because it is a discipline.

T4: You do have to discipline yourself.

T2: Even with this sheet has been a discipline, which I had not done before. But it's been a great help to organize behavior and participation. And eventually all are participating one way or another, all are speaking because when they retell stories they need to do it in Spanish, and I'm walking around the room evaluating on that. So, it's been interesting.

I: Great. S.?

T1: We all have our little things that work in the classroom. I think that participation, motivation, and discipline are all intertwined, as we've just said. I think it has something to do with attitude. If you are a beginning teacher, come into a classroom with a great attitude toward your job, about what you do and the students feel that. And I think the partici-pation and the want to participate not always for a grade come out naturally. They want to perform for you as you perform for them. I think as a first year teacher, you have to have that attitude. And again, I think teachers are born teachers—You have to have to project to them, "Yes, I'm going to learn to speak French, because my teacher loves, enjoys what she does and wants me to perform for her," and I think that in my classroom I have that projection, and, all our activities, and all the ex-ercises and everything all the group work—they do participate—I don't have to grade them every day as S. does, that works for her, I don't think it would work for me . . . it's a self-motivation thing. And most of my students are self-motivated. They do raise their hands, and partici-pate. And, I do want to say something about discipline. As a young, first year teacher, you will want to make friends with your students. Don't do it. Show them with your body language the first day that you may have a wall around you to start out with, that they won't get to close. Establish your rules. Make them known in the classroom. You're going to have discipline problems. Get your department chair, your principal involved. But respect them, and they'll respect you, and then you won't have any discipline problems. But it comes with time, it comes with experience, keep them busy with work. Give them homework every night. Tell them you're going to check it. Maybe not grade it every day but that you're going to check it, and that it's work you have to do. Inside the classroom, outside the classroom, and that's what you expect. Make sure you have these expectations and make sure the parents of your students know what you expect.

I: Do you tell them orally or you write them down?

T1: I tell them orally and write them down. And we have an open house at the beginning of the year where . . . our parents come to see us. So they know that there's going to be homework every night. They know what the textbook looks like. They know all of this. So, keep contact with parents. That will help let your principal know what you're handing out and what you expect and you won't have the discipline problems that you might have. Seek help. First year teachers usually don't get any help from anybody. Seek the help. Demand the help, and hopefully you won't have that problem, and always show that you like what you do. And then they'll respect you and then everything will flow smoothly.

I: Right. That's very, very true. And about expectations, I think they need to be reminded all the time that this is what we expect from them because they tend to forget it.

T1: I sometimes have to say, "Now, this is a . . ." go by the door and say, "Now this is an Honors class, isn't it?" You know, and go, "As opposed to a CP (college preparatory standard) class."

I: That's good. Good idea. Mr. G.?

T3: I have nothing to add that she didn't say, I believe, except that the attitude part is the big one. I came in to class and I'm all over the place and they just feed off of that. But if you come in the class and the first thing you say is in English and then two or three minutes goes by before you get your book out, and your lesson plans and your stuff, and you know, perfect chance to lose them. You're opening the door and inviting the problems. But if you're prepared, ready to go, you're not going to have any problems. And you can get them to want to learn French if they know that's what you're here for. And you know, you speaking French. I firmly believe it . . .

I: And how do you let them know that?

T3: I speak French. I come in and just go to it. And I don't do it nearly as much as I should. That's what you have to do. And that's true about having that wall . . . how friendly do you get? Because . . . they'll come up to you and ask questions and you know, and my personality is that I get friendly with students. It's just my nature. I'm involved in so many aspects of the school where I teach, from the football to the basketball game to junior class advisor—I've always got students coming to me asking me this and asking me that, and they know this about me, and they know that about me. And I've taken some with me to Europe and sometimes when you take them on a trip they see a different side of you, and so.

I: How do you build that wall, how do you present that in the first week of class?

T3: I think you've got to—you almost have to be halfway crabby.

T1: You have to be firm. But you don't have to raise your voice. And you have to show them in some way that you're concerned about them. I tell my students, "I want you to succeed. This is not a place where I want you to fail, and get 'F's. I want you to succeed," and if they get that feeling that you want them to do well, and that we as teacher understand them, that we are only one of six that they have, and I think it just comes out, that you show it.

T3: It's—You can't say it any other way. It's an establishment from day one. You can't get to October and then suddenly realize, "I should have done this. I'll start tomorrow."

I: The image that you give the first moment.

T1: They very first moment that they see you. That's when it has to happen.

T3: And they have to know what they're in there for, why they're in there.

I: It's just funny, I took my daughter—we went to Argentina this summer—my husband and my daughter, and we went to some schools there for her to visit. And the discipline was horrible there. Horrible, and she couldn't stand it, so she said, "How can they be working in such a noisy environment? And everybody talking at the same time?" So the kids really do benefit from the discipline. They do attempt to be disruptive, but . . .

T3: I see students who will get annoyed with other students . . .

T4: When they don't . . .

I: And my daughter is very talkative, she will talk at any time, but she felt the distraction of it. Being in such an environment—which it is, and St. Peters is very tight, more than other schools—but it's amazing . . . she's only eleven years old—to have that reaction.

T3: I've heard tell something about schools in France—different teachers have told me—they actually have some discipline problems occasionally.

I: You would see the teacher kissing and hugging the students—elementary, even the 6th and 7th graders. And you would never do that here. It's a different way of dealing with students.

T1: Yeah, you shouldn't touch the students. You might want to add to that wherever you end up as a first year teacher, your first job, that you make sure you understand all the policies. All the school board policies in your systems, so you don't do anything that might get you into trouble. All the rules. Make sure you read all the laws of discipline—the bylaws of your school, your county, so that you know about those. When you're given a handbook, read it from cover to cover . . .

T2: It's valuable information.

T1: Yes it is. You don't want to end up in court.

T4: You could end up requiring your students to do something and it might be against school board policy or something like that. I'd like to add to what S. and B. were just saying, and just say that it really is just so important to establish that image, if you can call it that, because that's really what we're talking about. The "image" of a French teacher, or Spanish teacher . . .

I: . . . and the reputation . . .

T4: . . . and reputation. You almost have to have a presence in the classroom. And because you are that way, the students are going to be motivated to be that way also, and you set an example yourself, by as S. said, respecting them and they will respect you. And also by other things as well. You're quiet when someone's talking and that shows them to do that. You model what you want them to do, and then they will do it. And you will be disciplined yourself and they will be disciplined. And you're just setting that tone so much by the way you are. And if you start class when the bell rings, and you're prepared, and you have that class going until the bell rings again, and you keep them busy the entire time. Kids get in trouble when they don't have something to do, when they're not occupied. If you don't have yourself together, and you're two or three minutes late getting class started, they have all this time to get involved with one another, and start talking, and so forth, that's when you have problems, is when you're not keeping them busy, and when you don't have yourself together, so, and that's hard as a first year teacher. It's very difficult. But if you can have your lesson plans structured in such a way that you have more than enough to do, so that you don't run out of stuff to do, and that you know yourself what you are doing almost every minute of that class period, that you're on top of it and keep things moving, and it keeps them focused and then you really don't have problems.

Let me make one more comment for interns. When you go into your internship, and walk into your teacher's room, that teacher already has discipline established when you go in there, that they've established from the beginning, and often times when you do your internship, you may not get a really true picture of what it's going to be like to be on your own, because those policies and all that have already been set up for you before you walked in. So when you walk into your classroom as a first year teacher, you do need to, at the onset, and I think S. said, make sure you set up these policies from day one, and that you go in there with a bang, ready to go, because since that was already done for you during your internship, when you go in, be ready to go, and have yourself ready to go, so you won't fall into that problem.

I: So we are also encouraging our students to come in, when they do the Senior I, the first day of classes, to see how all those rules, all those rules are put into place. Sometimes, because you start before we do . . .

T4: And you can't do that.

T1: That would be good—to get a video of the first day.

T3: I would invite you to come do that, that would be great. I love first day. I've even got their names memorized.

I: And the students . . . they usually don't see that because they start after. Excellent, great ideas, and I thank you so much.

SESSION #5

I: Here we are again, it's January 12th, and we'll be talking about advantages of block scheduling versus regular scheduling, particularly in Foreign Language teaching. So, who wants to start, the block schedule people? OK.

T3: I've been teaching now on block scheduling for . . . this is the third year?

T2: This is the . . . third.

T3: The third year, and . . . it has a lot of advantages. It has some disadvantages, too. So, it's not a cure-all for the ills of education. It does provide you with some neat opportunities. Being that you can, you've got to adjust your teaching methodologies . . . I approach it in segments . . . that's the best way that I've come up with it, plus it helps to be animated, and to involve the students as much as possible, so that they don't get tired or anything. I sometimes give them the 45-minute stretch, where they'll stand up and take a stretch and then sit back down. Sometimes I'll use that as an opportunity for them to—they have to say something to me in French to earn their seat back—then they can have their seat back. And that's a good five-minute break. Then we resume with wherever we were. Or that's a good transition point to go on to the next phase. I'm doing my French IV this semester, and I've got it mapped out that every day from 1:30 to 2 we speak, from 2 to around 2:30 we read, take care of grammar issues if we have any, then from 2:30 to 3:00 we're usually [doing] writing of some kind, whatever assignment I have given them. And then they ask me things about, "I want you to look over this and give me some pointers." The day they had to write a composition, there were two people talking, one asking, "Why haven't you been in school?" and find out why. They've got to tell them they've been sick or all this kind of stuff. Block scheduling I think, provides the opportunity to really get into the lesson without the threat that the bell's going to stop you, and sometimes it's amazing how much material you can cover in one day. Yesterday, in my first period class, yesterday we did a review session where we just spoke for a little. They took a quiz. They reviewed indefinite and definite articles. We put all the objects, the nouns they had learned, and we put them by . . . I made this giant *"un"* and this giant *"une"* and the *"un"* was on blue paper and the *"une"* was on pink paper, and we put all the objects beside of them and they told me all of those thing. Then, I pulled a cart out into the middle of the floor, and it had a book on it. And I put a calculator in front of the book, behind the book. I taught them their *"il y a,"* "there is," I taught them *"donc"* and then by the end of the class, they had told me *"la calculatrice est devant le livre, donc le livre est derrière la calculatrice."* And then I taught them the numbers from 20 up to 60, in addition to that, and we did all that plus take the quiz, and we did that in one class period. So it's like . . . (Snaps fingers twice)

I: You can cover a lot of . . .

T3: They've been in class five days, and they know nine questions. They know, *"Qu'est-ce que c'est? Qui est-ce que? Où est? Pourquoi? Combien de? il y a, donc,"* they know all the classroom objects, and today they learned *"être,"* the personal pronouns, and about twelve adjectives. And . . . you just keep moving and you just use it in all the different phases of the lesson, but you're constantly bringing things back up so it's just at a faster pace. But the time is there so it's not just hurled at them. And there's time to use it.

T2: Let me interrupt just a second. Using a textbook, which I'm not do-ing, but having done it in the past, I've been teaching on the block for 2-½ years, but one thing it does require you to do is to focus on what is really important in the lesson. And what is it that you want them to get out. So you have to know what's going to be . . . I know there's not really any fluff, but there's some textbooks that have some things that are utterly ridiculous. So you learn to pick and choose, and choose what's most appropriate and what will work best for your class. But you do have to carefully select your materials.

T1: I want to ask a question. When you were told three years ago that your school would go on block scheduling, were you not afraid, literally afraid, that your students would miss out on an extra 30 hours? That's the thing that I thought, and I guess what you're saying, that you have to pick out, you have to learn to pick out what is really, really essential in the lesson. Because there are a lot of things I know I teach that they could probably do without and do okay, maybe not all, but some of them. I guess we have to . . .

T2: But you refine that, you take it and maybe something you do at the beginning of class and have them finish it—something you go over. For my point of view, I do miss those 30 hours. But one thing that I do not like about block scheduling that was not made clear, I don't know, was because I wasn't there when it first started, first semester, but scheduling for us is terrible. You cannot be guaranteed consecutive semesters, even skipping semesters. Sometimes kids skip two semesters. Sometimes they skip a whole year.

I: Why is that?

T2: Because of . . . there's only 1½ French teachers and 1½ Spanish teachers and there's not enough to carry it. Now, enrollment is going up. I really see, I don't know about you, but, in the next year, we're going to need another language teacher. But because of the lack of teachers, and then also seniority, you have to put in who needs it most and so if the senior took Spanish I in the 9th grade, and he waited until his Senior year to take Spanish II, you know . . .

T1: I hope that students wouldn't do that.

T2: But you know, you would hope that, but, you know they do. Students do all kinds of things that you'd hope they wouldn't do. But scheduling to me is the biggest drawback we have . . . But I think that it could be done better. I had two students, the very first year of block scheduling, I had a class of French I the fall semester and it worked out that these two particular students in the room, by some miracle, or by some whim of the computer or whatever, or I think it may have been by their parents, just getting their schedules changed or something, they managed to get into the French II class the next semester. So, they were in French I from August to December.

T2: Were they Honors classes?

T3: No.

T2: See, only seniors can be guaranteed that they can get consecutive semesters.

T3: One was a junior, and one was a sophomore. And they got into that French II class that began in January. Well, that's unusual.

T1: Do you think there were some dealings under the table?

T3: Could have been, yes.

T2: Lots of string-pulling goes on.

T3: But my point is this: They, by May, had been in French one year, but they had taken French I and French II, and they knew more French than any student I've ever stood in front of. Their proficiency level. Because they had had it for an hour and a half for 180 days.

T1: That would be the only way that it would really be beneficial.

T4: Right.

I: And the administration didn't foresee that problem?

T2: Well, if they did, they chose not to address it. There are some schools that went on block scheduling only. And I see these are Foreign Language departments that have more influence than we do, but, I read this online in the FL Teach thing, that they went on block only if the administration guaranteed that they could do . . .

I: . . . sequence . . .

T2: . . . consecutive sequencing properly, and not skip a semester or two semesters, because it really is a big hindrance to your progression.

T3: Right now, I'm teaching my 90th French I student this year—I had 45 in the fall, and now I have 45. So that's 90 students who are enrolled in French I. And I taught all the French I this year. So their reasoning is, that if the 45 that I had in the Fall, that took French I, were immediately sent into French II, then this 45 right here are going to have to wait, because there's not enough teaching space.

T2: There's not enough teachers.

T3: But however, then again, if you have, under the old system, you would have room because you would have more classes.

T3: You'd have room for it, but in the block you don't. Because you have fewer sections.

I: Only three, right? Or four?

T3: Each teacher has three a day.

T2: And see, one of the problems that I don't think they anticipated is that now electives, which, we're a core-elective, they're in demand, and they need more electives than they need core.

T1: That's why they pull back for programs they've established which all our students to take not just six classes a year but eight classes a year. It was done for the students. It was not done for scheduling, it was not done for us. It was done to give them an opportunity to be exposed to more prospects.

T4: And really and truly, I believe that a lot of vocational areas you'll have behind—a lot of push on that, because it allows students to have time in their schedules to take a lot of their courses that otherwise they wouldn't take.

T3: Which may not be all bad.

T2: I don't know. Some classes are suited for block scheduling. And, I know of some schools that have gone to a split scheduling, do a block schedule in the morning, and maybe hourly classes in the afternoon, or vice-versa or whatever, but it's definitely not a perfect system. I'm lucky, I have third period planning, which comes at first lunch, and ends after second lunch. I have a two-hour block, which is nice, but when I think about what else I have to do, the work I have to do to catch up students, say in Spanish II or Spanish III, if they've missed a semester. I mean, I'm not there for me, I'm there for the students, and I hate to say it, but I would give that up again to go back to . . . or to some other kind of scheduling. I would not go to the A/B block, where you have one set of classes on Monday and another set of classes on Tuesday . . . now that sounds like a nightmare. I don't know who thought of that, but . . .

T1: Now, how do they do the English scheduling? If you take English I in the Fall, don't you have to take English II in the Spring?

T2: No. English II is your Sophomore year.

T1: So you just have English for one semester?

T2: Yeah, and one of the advantages is if you fail English I in the Fall, they schedule you immediately to take it in the Spring. But now, for example, all the AP classes are a year long, as is all U.S. history classes.

T4: Are they an hour and a half all year long?

T2: Yes.

T4: They're an hour and a half year long? That would be wonderful.

I: For the AP classes.

T2: But the history is interesting. You can fail Part One of U.S. history but still take Part Two, but you'd have to go back and take Part One and pass, if you passed the second part. Like I said, it's got its pros and cons—it depends on what you teach, who you teach.

I: Have you compared the results of the students completing one semester, not a whole year? But one semester, using the block schedule and then one year using the regular one?

T1: Your first semester French I, where do you finish in that Glencoe book?

T3: What happens is, I have a system that I've developed where I take that Glencoe book and I, let me tell you, I take that open-ended section where their intro starts, then I do Chapter 1 in its entirety, but I mix in Chapter 1 already, I taught "*être*" to "*des*." All right, I'm doing Chapter

1. Then I do Chapters 2 and 3 unbroken. When I get to Chapter 4—Family and the House, I also add in Weather and Summertime Actions, Winter Actions, too. So they can do the seasons of the year. So that they learn . . . I look at the chapter, and I say, "What are they learning in this chapter? They're learning how to tell the date," and then I say, "All right, well, let's teach them the seasons."

I: And that comes later?

T3: So then they learn seasons, so I say, "I want to get them to talk to me about the weather and the seasons, and some things they do. So Chapter 4 is a biggie for me. My folder is about that thick (gestures with arms) of Chapter 4 stuff. So then what I've done is I've taught Four and I've taught Chapter 9, so then I teach Chapters 5 and 6. Then I teach grammar and, I admit, I eliminate, I admit it, I eliminate the vocabulary of 7 and 8, trains and airport.

T1: But you can combine—they are so similar. Just like in Level II, I don't even do that chapter because we already did it in Level One, it's a repeat.

T3: So then I teach the grammar of 7 and 8. I mainly give them, I make sure they get regular "-ir" verbs, I teach "-ir" verbs in Chapter 5, I pull that from 7 back to 5 and then up, I make sure they get the big irregulars: "*mettre*," "*prendre*," all their families, and then the grammar of 9 is coming too, the vocabulary of 9 was taught in 4, and then I teach them clothing in 10, and then I teach them past tense in 13, and that's usually the course. That's usually the course.

T4: But you really do have to pick and choose because to me that's the thing with block scheduling and it's been my beef with it all along, that you're losing 30 hours of instruction, so you would have to eliminate some things.

T3: Oh, you do.

T4: There's no way you could get around it.

T3: The difference is, and I am getting ready to speak negatively about it, I know it sounds like I'm a proponent of it, and in some ways I am, but one good thing is: Chances are, when you get done with that Level I group, and they come, and let's say I have a Level II next year. Here comes the same crowd, and I know exactly what they were taught. I know exactly where to begin with them.

T2: If you get the same group.

T3: That's true. If I get the same group. . . . Sometimes I don't. But this year I did. Because it worked out that I taught all the French Is this year. The other teacher got the two French IIs and I got the IIIs and IVs. So I got levels I, III and IV, and the other teacher got the Level IIs. So, if you do get them, then you know where they are, and you know how to conduct a 2-week review and then you say, "I know I didn't teach you reflexive verbs in French I, and I know we did *'passé composé,'* but we didn't do *'passé composé'* with *'être,'* " so then you say, "I'm going to start there," and then you pick it up. Sometimes you're going back to that French I book, and you say, "We didn't do that, so let's put it in chapter whatever of the French II book," you have a plan. Negatively . . . the scheduling is not good. It is not good enough for them to wait six months . . . between levels. Amazingly, you'd be surprised at what they *do* know. You'd be surprised what they *do* retain. They retain more than I thought. But, not as much as they could.

T4: So not only are you losing 30 hours, but then when you get them back, you're back-pedaling to catch up.

T3: To an extent, yes. Block scheduling is also . . . it requires you to be creative.

T2: Constantly be on your toes, and you have to use several different ways, several different methods. I mean, you guys would do it anyway, your way, but if you don't, you are absolutely going to lose them. My biggest challenge, I find, is when we go from Level II above, because of a particular approach the other teacher who teaches Spanish takes. Lots of times, chances are she's had, like last semester, ⅔ of my Spanish II students I had not seen in Spanish I, and they were terrified to take Spanish II, just terrified, and I said, "Well, you know, don't worry about it." But then when you come to Level III, and if they've had this other teacher for Level II, they don't want to. I've had to beg kids to take Level III. And finally I'm talking them into it, and they say, "Oh no, we've had . . ." whatever, and I say, "No." I try to tell them it's going to be all right, but that's one of the things that happens, and that's not necessarily from block scheduling, but they, they've spent a whole semester in insecurity about being able to go on to the next level. I've talked to some students this week, this being our first full week back, about going on to Level III, and I knew they had had Level II with this other teacher, well, I don't know . . .

I: But that could happen to anybody, and in a way that's only a semester, and in the other system it's a whole year.

T3: I am, I found out. . . . And I feel like I'm hogging the conference.

T1: We're learning a lot.

T3: I have found out that in block, despite maybe some disadvantages, there are absolutely some awesome things that can go on in some individual class periods.

I: For example?

T3: There's some really neat stuff. You've got time to do some fabulous things and see progress like you've never imagined . . . for instance, today, I wrote some blanks on the board. I had taught them "*il y a*" and "*donc*" yesterday, and my lesson, [uses] taking attendance, too. It's not just something I do, it's a part of the lesson. Those kids are going to know how to count to 25 by heart by the end of the semester, because we count the kids. Every day, that's how we count role. I can't stand to walk into a class and stand just a second or two doing this (mimics silently taking attendance). I want to start when that bell rings. After that bell rings, I come in the door and I'm speaking French and we count every student. Today there were 18 in first period. So up on the board I wrote, "___ 18 ___ ___ classe ___ ___ 2 ___ ___" and then I pointed at it and just looked at it, and someone said, "*Il y a,*" and I wrote it and said, "*il y a,*" and pointed to the next part ("*dix-huit*") then somebody said, "*élèves,*" "*Il y a dix-huit élèves dans la classe . . . donc . . .*"—and someone remembered "*donc*" from the previous class—"*il y a deux élèves absentes.*" And then we did it, and I said, "Tenth day of class, and they get it," and so you can do so much with them. But like you said, that scheduling drives me nuts, because they walk out the door and I say, "That person could have done so much, but there they go out into the block scheduling blue yonder, and we'll see you in six months."

T2: The scheduling also leads you into a good situation with block. This semester I have Spanish IV with seven students first period and it just so happens that the woman who does computer graphics in our school who also has eight on-line computers has planning, so we've been going into her lab, we call it the computer lab, although that's not really what it is, and we've been going online, we've been establishing key pals, pen pals, we've researched articles on different Hispanic newspapers online.

T1: That would be wonderful.

T2: But if I had more than seven, I couldn't do it.

T4: And if she didn't have her friend . . .

T2: Yeah, so, of course I had to ask her, and ask our administrator, but it's wonderful, and I'm just so excited to have them. And I had all of them for Spanish III and most of them for Spanish II. In fact I have one who's technically a Level V because he managed to take Spanish II all semester before I got there and then Spanish II in the Spring when I got there. Then he took IV last Fall, and but, see it was IV last Fall, when he was one of three Spanish IV kids in a combined class with 15 Spanish IIIs and I had to put my IVs out in the hall, because they were true Level IVs but I lost them because I couldn't spend enough time with them and we just. . . . It was a nightmare.

T3: I hate combined classes. But I see now, I've got four French IVs, and you talk about having a class of FOUR . . .

T1: And you're allowed to have a class with four?

T3: Yeah. Under this system you are. There's no other choice. Either that or let me go to clean the bathroom or whatever. Clean the bathroom or teach French IV.

T4: We have to have twelve or they won't call it a class.

T2: Twelve?

T1: I have twelve in my AP and twelve in my Level IV, and Barbara gave me two classes. It's the first time it's ever happened. And it'll be the only time.

T4: I have nineteen in a combined Level IV and AP. Which is awful.

T3: So, my four kids, we go up, and like I say, we have an expression of the day, which is this little calendar I bought.

T1: Like the one you've got!

T3: Then, after the expression of the day, they've got to give me a sentence every day, and I keep a record of it every day. I keep a record of the sentence they write every day. And then . . .

T2: What does it have to be about?

T3: Anything. Just every day they have to provide me with a sentence. So I write their name, "Chris, Carol, Lewis, and Brandy," and I keep a record of their sentence, and I keep a record of their sentences, and every day, I mean, I'm going to fill up a bunch of folders, but there's their sentences. One of them was, *"Je ne suis pas contente parce que j'ai trois examens vendredi."* And another one says, *"Hier soir, j'avais trés faim, j'ai mangé un steak, des crevettes, mais je n'ai pas grossi."* And then Chris on the 8th, Chris's sentence was, *"M. G. va être très furieux parce que je n'ai pas mes devoirs,"*—I don't have my homework. So that's fun. And we start class with that every day.

T2: They write their sentences on the board?

T3: They've been just kind of telling them to me, and I've just been keeping a record. So we don't have any repeats.

T1: *"Je souhaite qu'il neige."*

T3: Yeah, 'subjunctif' . . .

I: That's neat. How do your students react to block scheduling? Any feedback from that?

T1: They probably don't know any other.

T2: Well, some of them don't. The present Junior class has just started block scheduling.

I: And they don't complain? They don't . . .

T3: Believe it or not, when we first changed, it was like, everyone was kind of excited, but also at the same time it was kind of like, it's like, you're going to expect everyone to . . . I was expected to go in and say, "Well, what do you guys think of this new schedule?" and stuff, and they were going to say all kinds of great things, and some were going to say, "Oh, man, this vacuums," and all this kind of stuff. Because they can't say that word in my class.

T1: We don't allow that word in my class, either.

T3: I don't use the "s" word in my class. So, they go . . .

T1: I taught you well.

T3: Yeah, you did. Good job. And so, but believe it or not, when I would ask they would say, "It's all right." (Shrugs shoulders) But I think that's partly adolescent opposition. But, there's some neat things you can do with block scheduling. And I tell you, I think probably at the bottom line, it may be best the other way for Foreign Language.

T1: That's the feeling we have, too.

I: The regular schedule?

T1: Yes. For us. For Science, maybe. For your vocational classes that have to [have] labs . . . it would be ideal . . . but for us . . .

T3: But I will say this, and I know I'm on the defensive, but I have become so used to teaching, and I'm kind of dynamic in class anyway, and so I've been able to get a lot of things done and I've got my system, and here I am talking as a selfish teacher—and my system set up that way, and friends, it was refreshing to see a new crowd come in there in January. It was the most refreshing thing for the whole school. And the discipline in our school was the best we've had—we haven't had any problems—everything went just as smooth . . . as it can possibly be.

I: That's true.

T1: It's ideal. It's an advantage to the students. The student who's a discipline problem is only a problem . . .

I: For one semester . . .

T1: . . . for one semester, and then the teacher can breathe and say, "Thank goodness he's gone."

T3: I don't know how much longer I could have tolerated the fifth period I had last semester. It was driving me crazy. I mean, they were the worst group I've had in seven years of teaching.

T1: Well, balancing both, if you were to select beginning next Fall if you had a choice, what would you choose?

T3: Well, I wouldn't know.

T2: You know what would be great, is to be, really to have the hour and a half all year long.

T3: Oh yeah.

T2: Like the AP classes are scheduled at our school. I think there you have so much to do . . .

T4: Too much.

T2: You can never have too much.

I: But if you didn't have the problem of scheduling . . .

T2: The scheduling. If we didn't have the scheduling problem . . .

I: Just with that idea, it's . . .

T2: If we didn't have the scheduling problem, it would be, because you do get used to that hour-and-a-half day.

T3: I have haunting memories of those last two years of the six-period day, when I had first period planning for the past two years, where at the end of the day I had taught five classes, and sometimes I didn't even know what I had taught. And I was, just . . . and I had a student teacher, and we just ran . . .

T1: That's my schedule. And mine is 6th period, so I start first period . . .

T4: Go five periods, so . . .

T1: And then 6th period, you don't have the energy, but I have the energy because I just get started in the morning and I get a lot done. I mean, I'm sure you get a lot done, but you don't have the energy to do it.

T4: Exactly.

T1: Yeah. I wouldn't mind trying it.

T4: One thing I wanted to ask you, is have you been doing it long enough to . . . and y'all don't have AP, do you?

T2: No.

T4: One of my concerns is that lack of 30 hours—how kids end up doing on those—of course, on the AP they get extra time, but like on placement tests, when they go off to school. Have you noticed any difference? Or . . .

T3: Not really. Not really. I've had some kids who place in areas really high, if you want to talk about other subjects, I know this is Foreign Language, but our EOC test stuff, we were exemplary.

T4: Do they take their end-of-course tests at the end of the semester? Are they allowed to do that?

T2: And the English tests that they're given, the competency tests that they're given, are given twice a year?

T1: Sixty-five percent of NC schools are on block scheduling, so they must . . .

T4: I'm hearing, though, I work in training with the Teacher Academy—and they're usually the cutting edge of things—I'm hearing that a lot of schools are going back, because there are so many disadvantages for a number of the disciplines, and Foreign Language is one of the main ones.

T3: And I would not doubt that in the slightest, and I would not disagree with it. I would say that probably, like say, when you ask those blunt questions, I'd probably say, "I don't know," but I'd probably be willing to go back.

T4: In my opinion, in the long run, it's better for the student of the Foreign Language to have the regular schedule. It may be better for the student of Science, to have block scheduling, but for the student of Foreign Language it's better to have regular scheduling.

T2: Because of the scheduling problems. Now, if you didn't have scheduling problems . . . then you'd expand your program. You'd have to. Then if you had a Freshman who took Spanish I starting their first semester, to go on . . . you'd have to open up, and expand. Or, at least advanced . . . we don't have that advanced, as far as the AG or AP, I think our classes, IIIs and IVs are considered AG, aren't they? (To T3:) Aren't they weighted . . . ?

T3: Yeah.

T2: But we don't have anything like that, but of course you need the many for the teachers you'd need to expand that program.

I: Do you also in those cases have a class limit?

T2: Technically, yes.

I: Twenty?

T2: Actually, no, it's twenty-eight. (To T3:) But did you know . . . has thirty-one kids?

I: Wow, even better.

T2: I had twenty-seven in my fourth period class last semester.

T3: I've had as many as twenty-seven.

T2: And that was a lot for a fourth period class. Because at the end of the day . . .

T3: I've got 22, 23, 20, and 25.

T4: And the limit is supposed to be what?

T2: Twenty-eight. The maximum.

T3: That's the same in almost any class.

T2: The standard. How many do you have?

T4: I have thirty-one in two classes.

I: Any other points in favor of the regular schedule?

T4: I think that language learning is more internalized if it is little blocks over a long period of times rather than big blocks over a short period of time. To me, students will learn it, and keep it, better. If it's this way, spread out over a long period rather than chunked in, to me that's a big advantage of regular scheduling.

T1: I sometimes feel rushed.

T4: That fifty-five minutes—it's kind of like you're constantly watching that bell, you know, "When is that bell going to catch me?" You know.

T3: And sometimes in block, you say, "When is the bell going to save me?"

I: You want the bell to ring, huh?

T3: But I tell you, it's nice to say, when that first class walks out and it's 9:40, to say, "The next class comes in at 11:25," you've got . . .

I: A large amount of time.

T3: A nice time frame there. You can actually go to the bathroom and wash your hands . . .

T2: . . . go to the library if you have to . . .

T1: In the regular schedule . . .

T3: . . . you can't breathe.

T1: . . . you couldn't breathe, and you know, you just start, and . . .

I: . . . and you have more students, also . . .

T4: . . . and when you have more students, you have more grading to do.

T3: It takes you much less time in block to get the six weeks averaging done. That's one of the biggest things. Being able to get that done really fast and turn it in.

T4: And I imagine grading papers is a lot easier because you have less students.

T3: But, theoretically also, they come sooner, they come in sooner intervals. I gave a quiz yesterday, I've got a quiz tomorrow, and I've got a test Friday.

I: So, more often. You give tests more often.

T2: Like my class through this semester, I've got 24, 4th period; 24, 2nd period; and 7, 1st period.

T4: Fifty-five students.

T2: Yes, that's it.

T3: I've got . . . forty-nine.

I: I've heard from a teacher, I don't know where in Eastern NC, that the problem in scheduling is in the Foreign Language program.

T1: I don't doubt it.

I: Have you seen that? Or . . .

T4: I would not doubt that.

I: They say it's killing the Foreign Language program in their region, with the block scheduling . . . and the problems with sequencing the courses.

T1: The students are discouraged. I mean, they can't get their classes . . .

T3: . . . until the next year. I would agree.

I: I guess they would just decide to take another elective.

T2: Unless they are the ones who are the college-bound ones. They'll at least get the two years. I don't know. I really haven't seen our numbers falling off so much, (To T3:) have you?

T3: Well, I've taken a tally of them, and out of a thousand students at Washington High School, we have taught 300-some. So 33 percent of every student there had taken Foreign Language.

T2: I can understand how that would happen, where it's killing the Foreign Language department, but I really haven't seen numbers . . . like I said, we have separate Level III and Level IV, and that's for French, too.

T3: I have seen a sharp increase in the number of Freshmen enrolled in the Level I Foreign Language classes, a sharp increase.

T2: Although Guidance keeps telling them, "Don't take it 'till your Junior year."

I: Probably—but do you think that's probably due to the block scheduling or to the teachers?

T4: They do it here, too. Guidance counselors do that.

T1: And some colleges require three years, and they can't do it, and they have to go to East Carolina—to their summer school class . . .

T3: I've got a class of twenty-four here and twelve were 9th graders.

T3: I respect the opinions there are about both of them, and the advantages there are to both of them; it's a hard position to be in.

T3: But let's shudder for the day they give no State EOC tests.

T1: No, I don't want to have to teach a test all year.

T3: And then you'd really be nervous about it, because you'd know at the end of the year the principal would be looking over your shoulder looking at your scores.

T2: They put so much of you on the line with that, do you notice? I think EOCs are not fair at all.

I: Anything else about block scheduling vs. regular scheduling?

T3: I'd say if you have a good teacher, like the four of us, that you're going to learn, regardless. If the child puts forth the effort, and the teacher does their best and puts forth the effort, there's going to be learning. It may not be ideal, but it's going to be learning.

I: Excellent. Good job. Now lets turn gears and go to discipline problems, the worst discipline problems of these expert teachers.

T1: I was a second-year teacher at Washington High School. I was teaching French, and I didn't have enough students for my schedule, so I taught an English class—the lowest English class you could find in the caliber of the students. It took me from September 'till the beginning of December to teach them that they *did* have to come to class with a book, with a pencil, and with some paper. So we accomplished that until December. There was a young lady . . . I will never forget her. I did not know what she had done to be on parole, but one day she decided that she was going to tell me what I could do with my book and my pencil and my paper. I was 22 years old, not much older than she was. And she developed an attitude at the time of the class, it was at the beginning of class. And I could see fire in her eyes, and I told her to sit down, and we would start our lesson, whether or not she had her book, pencil, or paper. And she got up, and she had a weapon on her, she had a knife. And she approached me with this knife and I was scared to death. I remember what I did, I screamed, and I went out the door to R., who was next to me, the tennis coach and Spanish teacher, next to me, I don't know if you remember him, but I went to him and said, "There's this student and she's going to stab me," and he said, "I'll take care of it." So I didn't do anything, but she was expelled—but it was very scary— I would say that that's the worst that could happen. And there are times to this day—this happened 30 years ago—that I still dream about it. Scary.

I: That was a scary moment for you.

T1: She had it about two inches away from my chin.

T4: How did you get away from her?

T1: I don't know. It all happened so fast, I don't know. I really don't know.

I: How lucky that you were able to go outside the classroom.

T1: So I went home, and my husband went to [the] . . . superintendent of Washington City Schools. He called him up and he said, "My wife is resigning. I don't know if you know what happened in her classroom, but she is resigning."

T1: Well, I went back the next day, but I couldn't resign, but that was one experience I'll never forget. It happens.

I: You see these things in the news.

T1: It happens, and that was a long time ago—when you don't expect anyone to carry a weapon in the classroom. So, that was my experience—not very pretty, but . . .

I: . . . very scary. Well, probably, would you call that a discipline problem?

T1: No, I don't think it was a discipline problem. It was just . . .

T2: . . . circumstantial.

I: Yeah.

T1: Because I had that class, after two months I had that class pretty much in control. In December we started learning things.

I: Oh, glad for that. B.?

T3: I've been trying to rack my brain to see which would be the worst. I have been fortunate—the Lord has blessed me that I have never had a great deal of problems—I've always been, kind of well liked by a lot of the students, and I've always been able to touch base with them. And one way for new teachers, and I've said this a lot, so it might be redundant, . . . that one of the best ways [for] new teachers is to get involved with other aspects of the school. Become visible, and the kids will gain a respect for you. So, like I am toying right this very minute with, "Am I going to drive back to Washington right now to announce the basketball game?" Because I am the stadium announcer for the games.

T2: "The Voice of Washington High School."

I: Wow.

T3: But anyway, that wasn't what you asked. But, get involved. But my worst discipline problem, believe it or not, was this last semester, and so that was the year seven of teaching. Should I say her name, because she's still around? Her name was Jane Doe, and she was a situation in which outside of the classroom, when you saw her, it was as if she was a relatively nice person. She always spoke, and said, "Hi, Mr. G.," and I'd go, "Hey, how ya doin'," but when she got in the class, she got off to a bad start. She started claiming that she could not understand what was going on, she said, "I can't understand this language stuff," and she said, "I don't know what you're doing." And then I would be up there explaining something in French, and then I would go and tell her, "This is what it means," and, "See how we put these together," then, "This is a question, this is how we make a question." And I would get down on her level, and she would, kind of, whatever, and then she would come in, and one day it might be head down immediately, and then, the next day it might be she's got both legs on her chair, you know how kids sit on their legs? You know, like that, she might be like this one day. (Demonstrates) And then, but she would also, right in the middle of class sometimes, go, "Eh!" (Makes loud disruptive noise) And then there would be this girl across the room who was her friend, who right in the middle of teaching would just start a conversation, sometimes under her breath and sometimes aloud.

T2: Across the room from each other!

T3: Yes! And I would go, "Whoa! What are you doing?" Well, I took her out of the room one day, and then, it was December the something-or-other, and she came into class, and teachers are human, and some days you can deal with it more than on other days, and that day I was, I don't know, I was uptight about something and she started, and she said, "I hate this class." (Puts head on desk) And then all of a sudden, real loud, she said, "This isn't fun, it's French!"

T1: That fired you up!

T3: And B. lost it, and I had to pray afterwards, because I got so angry, that I screamed at her at the top of my lungs and I told her to shut up.

T3: So I did not handle this professionally. But I was so mad I was shaking. And the next thing I did was I opened the door, and I said, "You're out of here." Well, the secretary of the school happened to have been walking down the hall as that happened, and she was like this in the hall, scared because she had heard me yell so loud, and I said, "You're out of here. Let's go." And she packed up, and I didn't even care that I had left the class. And I said, "Miss H. (the secretary), can you watch the class while I'm gone?" And she said (in a small voice), "Mmm-hmm." And she was two doors down and she could hear me.

T1: And everyone knows that you are not the type . . .

T3: No, I never . . .

T1: He must have really been angry.

T2: That was probably the first time he's ever sent anyone to the office.

T3: Well, about only the second, third maybe at most. Well, I marched her to the office and I said, "Have a seat," and by that time I was calm, or calmer, and I just picked up the discipline form and wrote on it, I quoted what she said, and I went to the administrator and said, "She needs to see you," and I said, "I need to see you." And I shut the administrator's door and I sat down, and I said, "I have not been very good." I said, "I have not been very professional." "This is what I said to her," I said, "if she comes in saying 'this is what he said to me' I want to own up to it, and say, 'This is what I said to her.' I told her to shut up at about 180 decibels," and she said, "Are you all right? Can you go back to class?" And I said, "I think I'll be all right," and I walked back to class calmly, and she was in in-school suspension during my class for the rest of the next week. She was supposed to have come back Monday, the last week of school, but she didn't. Something else for some other person, so she got in-school suspension another day.

I: So she had a reputation.

T2: Well, she never finished the course, really.

T3: Yes. Well, in six days she was back, on the day of the review, and so I reviewed with her.

T2: How did she do in your class?

T3: Believe it or not, the girl passed. Because of how she did on the final exam. She made a 68 on the final exam, and her overall average was 69.5, and I had to give it to her. I didn't want to give it to her. Believe me, I didn't want to give it to her. I said, "Well, the computer says 69.5, so . . ."

T1: Thank goodness for block scheduling—so you won't have to see her.

I: Yeah, that's right.

T3: But even there, if she'd see me in the hall, she'd speak, she'd say, "Hello, Mr. G."

I: And what would you say?

T3: I'd say, "How ya doin'?" like nothing happened. That's what you've got to do. You can't take it personally. And I remember, she even admitted to the principal, "I made him do it. I made him mad."

T2: She probably said it kind of proudly, because it's just her attitude.

I: Because she wants to be the mean girl.

T2: Yeah, I've known this child. I know who he's talking about, and she's had a terrible home life, and you have to take those things into consideration. It's not an excuse, but still.

T3: I'm not going to promote religion too much, but I would say go home and pray for the students, and you'll feel a lot better about them. You will feel a lot better about them.

I: You'll have more patience and all that . . .

T3: Yes.

I: And it's just an attitude that is not against you.

T3: You will be empowered to all then with a different set of eyes.

I: That's neat. C. or S., worst experience?

T2: I'll go. I'm like B., I don't really have a lot of discipline problems. Most of the time it's just talking, or . . . stuff like that, I can usually control. The worst discipline problem came up last Spring when S., my student intern, in that second period class. M. visited a couple of times, and it's unfortunate when you have an intern, because you want them to handle as much of the discipline as they can, because of what they're getting themselves into. But there was a situation in a Spanish II class, and over half the class were Seniors, and in their last semester. A lot of Senior boys, who pride themselves in just being the bad boys. There was one in particular who no matter where I put him—the rooms are only so big, you can only switch your seating arrangement around so much— and this one boy would manage to set up this situation in class, and there are some kids who do that, who set up a situation in class, and then remove themselves from the situation and watch the chips fall, and there was this one young man, and it took me a while to figure out who it was, because he was so good at it, he was so good at it he had never been sent to the office in his high school career, 'till I got him there. But you know, this child would say things under his breath to undermine . . . he'd started some of that when I was still in the class and had it, but when my intern came in, she had a hard time with it. He would say things under his breath, or pretend he was coughing, or deny he said something, or speak out of the back of his hand, just . . .

Oh, he was terribly annoying. We tried a number of things. To begin with, I spoke with him about the situation, and he said, "I know. We'll do fine," and then he was back to his old tricks again. And by then my intern had my class for the whole period—it was really getting to her, at one point, one time—and she was by herself at this point—and she knew exactly where I was, and she came to me and said, "I can't stay in there any more!" Oh, it was terrible. And I ended up, when I got the class back, we between the two of us had made some suggestions of what she could do, and she was real resistant to wanting to try some of these things, and I think she was scared. She was only a couple of years older than this guy, and so what I tried to do is, I said, "OK, let's try and work on everyone else around him, and get them not to be in ca- hoots with him." And that worked somewhat, but not long enough that it turned out to be a positive experience for her. I ended up having to do a contract with him. He was a Senior, he needed this class to go to college, so I ended up when I had the class back, with the assistant principal, working out a contract with him. He could do this, this and this, and he could not do this, this and this, and he had to sign it, his parents had to sign it. He had given me the wrong telephone number of his home to begin with, at the very beginning of school. That's illegal. So when I tried calling him, I got this guy who said, "Lots of people call for this boy here." So we got into this long conversation, I thought, "Oh my gosh, what have I opened up here?" Sometimes you don't want to get into this. You know, he got out of the class, he passed, but it was a long semester.

I: It was a difficult class. For the intern it was really a nightmare.

T1: And it's amazing how one student can ruin a class like that. The whole day.

T4: The whole chemistry of your class.

T1: Yeah.

T2: And so insidiously that you don't even know what's going on. I was able to pick up on who it was exactly after a while. After a while of not having to teach it but just sit back and observe, I could figure out who it was. But the intern up there, she's trying to remember to do her lesson plan. Particularly on days she was being observed, you know, it was tough for her.

She did, and it just happened to fall that way, and you get classes, where, like, you talked about developing personality, like from the onset they develop certain personalities and from the onset I was ready to get rid of that Spanish II class. Get my hands out of them. And I didn't even have them most of the semester, so that was kind of ironic, I thought they were the worst, and she taught them most of the time.

I: Yeah. Oh, S.

T4: I'm having trouble thinking of something.

I: Yeah . . .

T4: I really, as the others have said, I really don't have any discipline problems, and I'm . . . probably the closest thing that would be recent is last year I had a student who was in Spanish III, and she tended to be pretty emotional, and she was a poor student. She really struggled for her grades. And there was a day, and as a matter of fact I think my intern was observing on a day I think she was acting up a bit. I returned some test papers, and she promptly wadded the test up, threw it on the floor, and just decided she would leave. And I'm standing there looking at her, "Well, OK . . ." She's got her books and I followed her out of the room—I knew [my intern] was sitting there, and it was a good class anyway, so . . . I could leave them by themselves anyway—And I told her she would either have to come back in the class or she would have to go . . .

I: . . . to the office . . .

T4: . . . to the office, one or the other, or she could come in here for a few minutes, in this office area, if she just needed a minute to calm down. But that she could not act that way in class, and that she would never ever do that again in my class. And she never did . . . and she ended up coming in here.

I: By herself.

T4: I said, "Your choice is, come in here, come back in class or go to the office." And that really the best option would be to sit in here and cool off a minute, "Because you're just not going to be allowed to act like that, ever. You just may not do that. And frankly I think you owe the class an apology." And so, she stayed in here the whole period, and I came back at the end of the period and made sure she was still in here. She was fine by then, she just had a blow-up.

I: Did she apologize to the class?

T4: She did, she came back in and apologized and she was fine. And there were times during the year that she did not react. She did not wad it up and she did not throw anything and stomp out of the class. So she never did that again. But you could see her body language—she might want to do something. But she wasn't going to do that again. And now, at the age I am now, I don't ever raise my voice at a student . . . (To T3:) I have done it when I was younger. But keeping your voice calm if a student is upset is very . . . is a good thing to do. I can think . . . it was a number of years ago when we were first integrating our schools, that there would be problems that would erupt in class, and it didn't have to do with what was going on in class but what was going on outside of class. And I had a student pick up a desk and throw it across the room at another student in the middle of class.

I: My goodness!

T4: And again, it had nothing to do with anything that I was doing in class, but it had to do with all this stuff that was going on . . . and all this anger that was boiling between them. And I did yell that day. I immediately went and opened my door so hopefully someone else would hear what was going on, I didn't want to leave, and I yelled. And I had a guy in the class who was relatively large, and he grabbed the one who was throwing the desk long enough that I could call someone to get them in there to help.

I: That's scary.

T4: That's probably as far as physical things the only thing I could think of, but, I mean, I'm like B. If you have a relationship with the students, if you see them somewhere besides in the classroom . . .

I: . . . they do respect you.

T4: They respect you, they know that you're a person, that you're human, that you have problems, too. And I just think they accept things from you better. And we talked before about letting them share things about what's going on in their life better, where you know things about them and you just don't have the problems. You just don't. I just don't have discipline problems.

T1: And I just want to add just a little bit more about that: that they know you really care about them. That you take an interest in what they do—in their school life and their home life—and you don't go out of your way to do that, if you just . . . just a couple of questions here and there will do it. And then they think, "Well, you know, they might really care about us," and then they'll perform for you and respect you and you won't have any problems.

T4: That's right.

T1: One incident I just remembered, and this was a student of mine, it's been years ago, but I was returning a really important paper back to them. It was a test that they had taken, and it was a combination of a lot of different things they had done, and it was a really important test. And one girl had not performed well, and she had not studied, and she really didn't like the class anyway, and so she tore it up—first, she tore it up two times and then wadded it and then threw it in her book bag or wherever she threw it. I ignored it. We had gone over the test and made our corrections. Then I said, "Oh, pass back your tests, and if you've made your corrections like you were supposed to then you'll get some extra points." And that cured that.

T2: Were you going to do that anyway?

T1: No, I saw her do it, and so she stomped out of the classroom, and the next day she was fine.

T3: I remember . . . preventative maintenance is a very good thing. I remember one day I was getting ready to give a quiz, and I had turned around and was looking across the room, and I saw a student writing answers on her desk as fast as she could. She was writing all the answers and it was as if I saw it and I just went, "OK B., whatcha gonna do?" And so I turned around to the board, and I was writing something on the board pertaining to the quiz. And I said, "Guys, I'm going to do a desk check, just out of the blue, in about two minutes. And I'm going to keep my back turned, so you won't be accused, and if there's anything you think I could accuse you of, I want you to be sure you erase it." And I just stood there writing.

And two minutes went by, and I go through and checked every desk and it had been erased. So we avoided the cheating by not ever letting it happen. And that's what I do about the bathroom across the hall from my room. I go in there, and they know I'm coming. Any time between the change of class and they know I may go right in that door and come right back out, but . . .

T2: That ends the smoking problem.

T3: It ends the smoking problem.

T2: Has L. been doing this too?

T3: Yeah, it's been a lot better.

T1: You need to come to our bathroom. Did you ever talk to the girl who was writing? After the fact?

T3: I probably should have, but I didn't, because it had never happened before.

T1: I will write them little notes.

T4: And there, that's another thing preventatively you can do, like if you know you have a student who's emotional like that student I had. If she got a bad grade, I would write her a note and say, "So-and-so, I know you probably studied for this, come talk to me if you don't understand this," or whatever, and then you can avoid some of those problems, rather than just . . .

T2: That's part of that personal contact, because they just appreciate that.

T4: That's right. They do.

T2: And like all of you were saying, it takes like a minute and a half to put a little note . . .

T3: I start my classes off every year (the French I classes) with a diagnostic test, just to see where they're at. There'll be an English sentence and I'll just say, "Underline the subject, circle the verb," or whatever. Then I'll have questions like, "Tell me your favorite activity. Tell me everything I would have to know to begin that activity as a complete layperson," and they'll write and write, because it's the first day of school and they'll want to impress the teacher. And then I'll go and read them, and I'll put comments on as many tests as I can. I'll say, "I play the piano, too," or, "Did you see France won the World Cup this summer?" for all the soccer crowd . . . and they were writing, "My favorite sport is soccer," and they immediately, they get their papers back and you've written stuff on it and it's like . . .

I: They like to read it.

T3: It's like it's the most important thing ever written, and they're reading what you had to say about it.

T1: Those French I students that you don't know.

T4: Any time you write comments on students' papers, I think it's just, you know, if they've been asked to write something personal, and they happen to include something. This year we were writing about families, and this girl happened to write about her mother being sick for an extended period of time, and so I wrote her a long note, and she came back to me later and said that it just really meant a lot to her. There was a student who lost her mother, and she wrote an essay, and I can't remember now, but she wrote something in her essay about her mother, and about the fact that her mother was no longer there, and I wrote her a note back, because I lost my mother when I was in high school also, and I explained that to her.

I: You shared that with her.

T4: I shared that with her, and that sort of thing makes a big difference.

T1: (Reaching out to T4) Are you OK?

T4: Oh yeah, I'm fine, I'm fine.

I: Makes more of a difference than you would think.

T4: (Agrees)

I: But you need to show the human side of the teacher.

T1: Oh, yeah, some students don't think we're human at all. I wonder why that is, why is that?

T3: Because they see you in an institutionalized position. And ever since they've been five years old, there's been an adult there "who tells me what to do" or "who gives me this and makes me learn it."

T4: And I think there are some teachers who are that way, and who are not human—that could be one of the reasons, too.

I: (Agrees)

T3: That's another thing I don't like about these data-driven, test score Almighty from the State Department, or Raleigh, or [the] Legislature. They forget that we're working with human beings. Don't ever forget that when you're teachers (Points to camera), we're working with human beings. That's the whole thing of school. Is the human touch, and if you lost it, no job!

Others: That's right.

T1: You're missing the ride.

T3: That's right.

I: And the effect of teachers on students is so strong . . .

T4: It's absolutely amazing . . .

I: Amazing . . .

T4: Sometimes that they will come back years later, when they come back to visit and you'll see them somewhere, and there's something that happened in your class, or that you've said that they just hang on to. It's amazing. How much influence we had on them.

T2: And you don't think you had any at the time.

T4: That's right, and you don't think we had any.

I: Good. Good ideas and thoughts.

SESSION #6

I: OK, today is the 28th of January, and we'll be talking about lesson plans, Who'll start? S.? All right.

T1: Oh, where do you start when you do . . . I know what my lesson plans are every day, but as far as planning lessons, we experienced teachers don't go through the motions of a six-point lesson plan, we do that automatically. So I guess it will be hard for us—all of us—to talk about lesson planning. But, here we go. I think as a first-year teacher, you need to be very familiar with your standard course of study. So that you know what in your curriculum you have to cover. You are accountable for teaching what is in that book that your system gives you. So whatever it is, you need to study it carefully. And I guess you go from there, and you take that, and you take your textbook, and you decide how many weeks you have in a year, or in a six-weeks or nine-weeks, and you divide up the materials so that by the end of the year you have covered all that you were supposed to have covered. And you have to take into consideration meetings and fire drills and testing that is taking place outside your classroom, that is pulling kids out of your room, things like that. But with experience, every year you're going to find out new things about lessons planning, but with experience you will be able to juggle your textbook and your course study plan and figure out what to teach. But that's on a broad basis.

I: Yes.

T1: On an everyday basis . . . you need to find ways to . . . foreign language is an elective. So you need to find ways to recruit your clientele—so you need to make it as interesting as possible. So you need to find some warm-up activity that will settle the students down and make them interested in what you are trying to teach them. You need to always review what you did yesterday. Either through homework, or "what did you do in class yesterday?" Whether it's in English or in the target language. And then you get to the crux of the lesson, which will probably take 25 or 30 minutes, something like that. Then you have to have closure. You have to make sure that they know what their homework is, and that they're going to anticipate all the fun things that they're going to do the next day. So that's basically how I plan.

I: All right. I know that with experience you don't sit and write down every single thing you're going to say in class.

T1: But I do write down what I'm going to do—even to the hand-out I'm going to pass out, because I'm going to forget to hand it out. And what the homework is. I always write out what the homework is. When you're assigning tests, always write that out. Even the lesson itself. If the lesson is going to be about the use of "*a*" and "*le*" in Spanish, it's "*a le*" and in French it's "*au*," write a little note as to how to get into it, or samples, or little post-it notes as to what to tell the kids. What worked last year might not work this year, but what didn't work last year you need to change a little bit. So there are all kinds of things that first or second year teachers will learn through experience. What to do and what not to do. And each class is going to be different. You might teach French I all day long and have 5 different classes. So you have to adapt . . .

I: Make adjustments . . .

T1: Make adjustments so that your class works, so they'll learn it one way or another.

I: Good.

T1: Is that specific enough?

I: Yeah, great.

T1: And I'm sure both of you do basically the same things.

T4: We do, we do. I've got a plan book. Just so you can see kind of what we do. This is Level II, this is Level III and these are the upper levels, which are the levels that I teach. And this is Monday, Tuesday, Wednesday, Thursday, Friday. And Friday of this particular week I opened to was a teacher work day, so I didn't plan anything for that day. But basically, for example, on Monday . . . you can see that for each day I have "HW" written, so that's homework, so that every day I know what the homework is for a given day. If someone's absent, we have something to refer back to—it's just a good idea to have it in there. And basically I'm like S., I don't put how . . . I don't really say how I'm going to cover that, in my mind, and I know by experience how I'm going to go about doing it. So basically all I have in here is, "Review page 207, Go over homework, Read an extra page here, Explain this page, and F&G and Homework." So to somebody it may look like, "Well, what in the world is that?" But I know what it is.

I: Have you already prepared your lesson for tomorrow?

T4: Yeah.

I: The interesting thing would be for you to open a book, and see what you have to cover, and think out loud. Would you mind doing that?

T1: What I do, I do it all on Sundays. I spend all day Sunday planning for my week, OK? And I write down everything I want to do that week. No Monday, Tuesday, Wednesday, Thursday, it's everything I want to do that week. And then I check off everything we've done. And then we have tapes, we have workbooks, we have text . . . we have extra handouts. I want to make sure I get all of that covered.

I: And you get all the text, the handouts, the tapes on that Sunday?

T1: I do all my work at home.

T4: Absolutely.

T1: We have tape books, we have a teacher manual, and I need to know where my tapes are, I need to know what exercises we're going to do . . . so you put in the tape and it's ready to do. And they're in order, so I don't have to look for them. And I always jot down what their homework is, and their workbook. We often use the workbook for homework. And I do all of that. And I'm at the point that whatever I want to do that entire week, most of the time, I get it all done. Unless I've been distracted. And that could happen. But that's usually how I do it.

T4: And if you have, if you kind of have an idea of where you're going. . . . A lot of time I'll do several weeks at a time. For example, if you know a holiday is coming up, and you don't want to get caught on that holiday right in the middle of something, then you might want to jump ahead and kind of map out where you're going so that you know where that's going to fall. I always try to have my tests posted at least a week ahead of time.

I: So they know.

T4: So they know exactly what's coming up and when it's coming up . . . and if you have your lesson plans sketched up, however sketchy they may be, then you know, you kind of know what direction you're going. You know in mine, I already have meetings I'm going to have, students that are going to be out for school-related events, it's kind of like . . .

T2: It's like a journal, really . . .

T4: It really is, because you're going by . . . you're kind of going by it . . . and it's not the Gospel, as S. said, but there are some times when something comes up, and you need to address whatever that something is. Like a teachable moment, or whatever it is . . . but most of the time, you've got your week mapped out. And I pretty much stick to my week, too. Once in a while I'll have something that won't work out, but most of the time whatever I've mapped out, it's right exactly where I am. Now I usually do this on Thursdays . . . but that's just a difference . . . because at that point I've already got through what I need to get through for the week, and I want to know where I'm going for the next week. So if there is going to be a test that next week, I can go ahead and let them know. So I like to do mine on Thursday. But I do the same thing, like if I have any worksheets written on here.

I: For the whole week?

T4: For the whole week. So that if I'm giving any tests, I get that copied and run off, I get my tapes lined up so that you are prepared. You don't want to go into class and not know where your tape is. You've got a tape you want to listen to, and you have no idea where it is, and it's not cued up, and it would take class time to find it, and you have discipline problems when you do that. You're going to have a problem. You have to be ready when that bell rings, with everything you need where it needs to be, and you can put your hands right on it.

T1: What I do, if . . . we're really working on specific vocabulary for a couple of days, three days or a week, instead of having the vocabulary in my head, which I may forget, or on paper, I have it in my plan book. And I have my plan book open, and I know I've got all the vocabulary here, listed so that I won't forget my notes.

I: How do you plan the "how to do it"?

T1: How you do it is in your head.

I: But what happens in your head?

T1: What happens in my head? I do think about how I want to present a lesson.

I: Tell me about it.

T1: I want to do it orally. I can't . . . Give me a topic. (Confers with T3) Teaching how to tell time. Well, telling time . . . You've got a clock. I've got a felt clock with felt hands, And I look at my watch and say, "*A quelle heure la classe de français commence-t-elle? Quand est-ce que . . . A quelle heure est-ce-t-elle commence? La classe de français, à quelle heure est-ce qu'elle commence?*" They know the verb "commence" and we look at the clock.

T1: Yes. Especially in French I, I always give them . . . I always say a lot of things, and they have no idea what I'm saying, because they don't have much vocabulary. I haven't taught them, so, French I is hard, because you're saying things, and they give you this blank look. "You mean you haven't had that yet?"

T3: And I'll say, Today, "*est-ce que . . .* " and they don't know about "*est-ce que.*"

T2: They can ask.

T1: It just goes on in your head while you're doing it.

I: You're rehearsing it?

T1: Yeah, you think about it. And you say, "How can I present this lesson?" Present it orally first. Even if they don't know all the vocabulary. "We're going to do numbers now. We're going to count from one to twelve. But we're going to stop at eleven, because we don't say '*douze.*' We're going to say '*midi*' and then have a sun or something, and say '*minuit*' and have a moon."

I: Do you practice questions that you will ask your students? Or do you think of questions you will ask them?

T1: Oh yeah. You can ask them to repeat over and over. Sometimes I write them down on little post-it notes. The more examples you have . . . you can't always have all the examples you want in your head, as you're teaching something. Especially if it's a harder concept. You've got to refer, "What are some of the things I can ask them?" and put them on a post-it note, and have lots of examples.

T2: One thing I was going to say, and I was going to address block scheduling lesson planning as opposed to your year-round. What the TPRS method—particularly in the Spanish I level—you present vocabulary, just listen to begin with, and you mime, you scream, you shout, you cry. Today, someone who comes in my 2nd period class for 3rd period said that it sounded like a gorilla having a baby in the hall, when they were at the door. So you get them as involved as possible so they don't repeat anything. You practice with each word. And you have maybe "point," "*Señala*," and you've got to think of all the things, and sometimes you can't remember so you have to write all those things down. You do stuff with your elbow, and you do stuff in the air, and it just helps to write stuff down. Sometimes, all of a sudden, my mind just goes—(gestures with hand). I have no idea what's going to come next. You have to write some of those things down. But a lot of things, particularly in your upper-level classes, you find you don't have to repeat that much. You've done it so many times. And you might do a variation, to adapt it to each class. And like you've said, what works in one class might not work in another. So you may have to use a different strategy. And you make note of that. Because you may forget what kind of adaptation you've made. Because it might apply to another class later on down the road.

T1: Or, you may say, "Scratch this, I'll never use this again."

T2: For block scheduling planning, you almost do two lesson plans in one day. Depending on what you're working with, some things take longer to absorb and digest. So you may just get through the directed work, where you're working and we have an hour and 50 minutes as opposed to your 50 minutes. So I have found if you go any farther than the 25 or 30 minutes as far as what the presentation is, then you cannot stand in your class and just lecture for 90 minutes. It's boring to you. But it's [more] difficult to transition to that than you might think.

T4: I'll bet.

T2: And it's very difficult—I know older teachers who have taught for lots and lots of years and years have a hard time making the transition.

It's just very difficult to change. But you have to keep lots and lots of activities. You want to have lots of different types of activities you want to have them up and around, sometimes for a break, but mine are up and around so much they're complaining about being up so much. I have them hopping and jumping and screaming and shouting and crying and laughing. And you can over-do that kind of thing too much. But it's really a fine thing to balance your activities and keep them interesting.

T4: I was going to show you, I'm getting ready to start this new chapter, actually. I'm getting ready to start on my lesson plans for this chapter, and basically what I would do, the process I would go through, would be first of all to correct it in my mind to the whole unit. And this whole unit was called, "One day." The chapter we just finished was, "What do you customarily do?" So the chapter I'm getting ready to start will be, "What are you going to do this weekend?" In my mind, then, I'm thinking, "What can I pull in that the students will be interested in, from the newspaper, what can I get from the magazine, what about some movies, what about TV schedules?" Because the subtitles here are listed, "A magazine," and, "I'm inviting you to a party."

Notes

1. East Carolina University has implemented the Senior Year Experience since 1996. The purpose of this year-long internship is to provide prospective teachers with a more realistic view of teaching in American schools. Students under this requirement take a number of block courses and work with their assigned clinical teacher one full day once a week during the first semester of the senior year. The block courses are FL methods, advanced psychology, advanced technology, and a special education course. The work in the school includes primarily observation of teaching practices and extensive dialogue and reflection with the clinical teacher. During the second semester of the senior year, students complete their internship which requires them to teach throughout the entire semester including three consecutive weeks of full-time teaching. In addition, students complete a teaching portfolio that follows the same guidelines that the performance-based assessment instrument requires of teachers during their first three years in the profession. The advantages of this experience are primarily the opportunity it provides students to gain first-hand insight into the teaching profession and a longer exposure to the school system. However, a number of problems have arisen since its implementation, namely, problems with student retention in the program. Students get the impression that the demands are overwhelming and some prefer to switch to the non-teaching degree and seek licensure via an alternative route such as lateral entry. Further evaluation of the senior year experience is needed in order to assess its value short and long term.

2. The term "clinical teacher" is used here in lieu of the more traditional "cooperating teacher." The former is preferred to be consistent

with the terminology that the School of Education at ECU has adopted in its newly revised Teacher Education Programs.

Likewise, the term "intern" is used instead of "student-teacher" for the same reason.

3. Schools' Partnership Grant and BellSouth Foundation

4. Other topics were discussed with the participating teachers, but are not included in this analysis. The author selected those topics that were of more concern to FL interns and beginning FL teachers. However, the complete transcription of the interviews is included in Appendix D for those readers interested in the teachers' beliefs on other topics such as block scheduling and lesson planning.

5. East Carolina Foreign Language Educators' Collaborative (EC-FLEC), an organization sponsored by the Department of Foreign Languages and Literatures, ECU, that serves foreign language teachers (K–12) from eastern North Carolina. Meetings are held from 9:30 A.M. to 1:00 P.M. at ECU/Rose High School six times per academic year. Teachers receive one-unit renewal credit. This organization has been recognized by the Department of Public Instruction and the Foreign Language Association of North Carolina.

6. The following hypotheses and corollaries summarize the Proficiency Movement (Omaggio Hadley, 1993, p. 77).

Hypothesis 1: Opportunities must be provided for students to practice using language in a range of contexts likely to be encountered in the target culture.

Corollary 1: Students should be encouraged to express their own meaning as early as possible after productive skills have been introduced in the course of instruction.

Corollary 2: Opportunities must be provided for active communicative interaction among students.

Corollary 3: Creative language practice (as opposed to exclusively manipulative or convergent practice) must be encouraged in the proficiency-oriented classroom.

Corollary 4: Authentic language should be used in instruction wherever possible.

Hypothesis 2. Opportunities should be provided for students to practice carrying out a range of functions (tasks) likely to be necessary in dealing with others in the target culture.

Hypothesis 3: The development of accuracy should be encouraged in proficiency-oriented instruction. As learners produce language, various forms of instruction and evaluative feedback can be used in facilitating the progression of their skills toward more precise and coherent language use.

Hypothesis 4: Instruction should be responsive to the affective as well as the cognitive needs of students, and their different personalities, preferences, and learning styles should be taken into account.

Hypothesis 5: Cultural understanding must be promoted in various ways so that students are sensitive to other cultures and prepared to live more harmoniously in the target-language community.

7. An overview of the development of the ACTFL Proficiency Guidelines should be of interest to the reader. With the creation of the President's Commission on Foreign Language and International Studies numerous public and private groups worked together to set the future directions for the FL profession (Hiple, 1987). The task was mainly to set nationally-recognized proficiency standards. This was initiated with the work done by the Modern Language Association (MLA) and the American Council of Learned Societies (CALLS) in 1977. These organizations obtained support from the Rockefeller Foundation and the National Endowment for the Humanities to form five task forces: "1. the Task Force Institutional Language Policy, 2. the Task Force on the Commonly Taught Languages, 3. the Task Force on the Less Commonly Taught Languages, 4. the Task Force on Public Awareness, and 5. the Task Force on Government Relations" (Hiple, 1987). These task forces' work was to offer our profession "a unifying principle, a sense of mission, and a set of educational objectives on which to focus its energies" (Brod, 1980, p. 4).

In 1981 ACTFL initiated to work on language proficiency activities and received funding for two projects from the U.S. Department of Education. One project was to offer academic oral proficiency tester training, the other was to "respond to the commission's charge of creating 'language proficiency achievement goals' and was undertaken in collaboration with the Modern Language Association" (Hiple, 1987, p. 8). In 1982 the ACTFL Provisional Guidelines were circulated at the ACTFL Annual Meeting in New York and in 1986 they were revised and made available for implementation: "These guidelines identify stages of proficiency, as opposed to achievement, they are not intended to measure what an individual has achieved through specific classroom instruction but rather to allow assessment of what an individual can and cannot do, regardless of where, when, or how the language has been learned or acquired. . . . These guidelines are not based on a particular linguistic theory or pedagogical method, since the guidelines are based-based, as opposed to based-based, and are intended to be used for global assessment" (ACTFL, 1986).

8. The North Carolina Second Language Standard Course of Study (1999) was revised in 1999 to be in alignment with the Standards for Foreign Language Learning. The new course of study is organized grade by grade and course to course. It targets seven broad goals (Interpersonal Communication, Interpretive Communication, Presentational Communication, Cultures, Comparisons, Connections, and Communities). It fos-

ters integration of skills and includes the addition of strands. The seven goals are:

Interpersonal Communication: "The learner will engage in conversation and exchange information and opinions orally and in writing in the target language" (North Carolina Revised Second Language Standard Course of Study, 1999).

Interpretive Communication: "The learner will understand and interpret written and spoken language on a variety of topics in the target language" (North Carolina Revised Second Language Standard Course of Study, 1999).

Presentational Communication: "The learner will present information, concepts, and ideas to an audience of listeners or readers on a variety of topics in the target language" (North Carolina Revised Second Language Standard Course of Study, 1999).

Cultures: "The learner will gain knowledge and demonstrate understanding of the relationship among practices, products, and perspectives of cultures other than his own" (North Carolina Revised Second Language Standard Course of Study, 1999).

Comparisons: "The learner will develop insight into the nature of language and culture by comparing his/her own language(s) and culture(s) to others" (North Carolina Revised Second Language Standard Course of Study, 1999).

Connections: "The learner will acquire, reinforce, and further his/her knowledge of other disciplines through the foreign language" (North Carolina Revised Second Language Standard Course of Study, 1999).

Communities: "The learner will use and/or demonstrate cultural knowledge and understanding within and beyond the school setting for personal, educational, and professional growth and enrichment" (North Carolina Revised Second Language Standard Course of Study, 1999).

Bibliography

American Council on the Teaching of Foreign Languages, 1986. "Proficiency Guidelines." Hastings-on-Hudson, NY: Author.

American Council on the Teaching of Foreign Languages. 1993. "Provisional Guidelines for Foreign Language Teacher Education." In G. Guntermann (ed.), *Developing language teachers for a changing world* (pp. 213–27). Lincolnwood, IL: National Textbook Company.

American Council on the Teaching of Foreign Languages. 2001. ACTFL.org.

Armstrong, K. M., and C. Yetter-Vassot. 1994. "Transforming teaching through technology." *Foreign Language Annals* 27 (4): 475–86.

Barasch, R. M., and C. V. James. 1994. *Beyond the monitor model: Comments on current theory and practice in second language acquisition.* Boston, MA: Heinle & Heinle.

Belanger, J. 1992. "Teachers as researchers: Roles and expectations." An annotated bibliography. ED342751.

Brod, R. I. (ed.). 1980. *Language study for the 1980's: Reports of the MLA–ACLS language task forces.* New York: Modern Language Association.

Cadierno, T. 1995. "Formal instruction from a processing perspective: An investigation into the Spanish past tense." *Modern Language Journal* 79: 179–93.

"Carnegie Classification: The Carnegie classification of institutions of higher education." Carnegiefou...cation/CIHE2000/defNotes/Definitions.htm.

Chomsky, N. 1965. *Aspects of the theory of syntax.* Cambridge, MA: MIT Press.

Cohen, L., and L. Manion. 1985. *Research methods in education*, 2d ed. London: Croom Helm.

Cook, V. 1996. *Second language learning and language teaching*. New York: Arnold.

Crooks, G., and P. M. Chandler. 2001. "Introducing action research into the education of postsecondary foreign language teachers." *Foreign Language Annals* 34 (2): 131–40.

Curwin, R. L., and A. N. Mendler. 2001. *Discipline with dignity*. Upper Saddle River, NJ: Merrill.

East Carolina University Research Symposium. 1998. *Resources for action research in education*. Greenville, NC: East Carolina University–School Teacher Education Partnership.

Eckman, F. R., D. Highland, P. W. Lee, J. Mileham, and R. Rutkowski Weber (eds.). 1995. *Second language acquisition: Theory and pedagogy*. Mahwah, NJ: Lawrence Erlbaum Associates.

Ellis, R. 1990. *Instructed second language acquisition*. Cambridge, MA: Basil Blackwell.

Ellis, R. 1994. *The study of second language acquisition*. Oxford, England: Oxford University Press.

Ely, C. M. 1994. "Preparing second language teachers for strategy instruction: An integrated approach." *Foreign Language Annals* 27 (3): 335–42.

Ervin-Tripp, S. M. 1974. "Is second language learning really like the first?" *TESOL Quarterly* 8: 11–128.

Gallaway, C., and B. J. Richards. 1994. *Input and interaction in language acquisition*. Cambridge, England: Cambridge University Press.

Galloway, V. 1987. "From defining to developing proficiency: A look at the decisions." In H. Byrnes and M. Canale (eds.), *Defining and developing proficiency: Guidelines, implementations, and concepts* (pp. 25–73). The ACTFL Foreign Language Education Series. Lincolnwood, IL: National Textbook Company.

Gardner, R. 1985. *Social psychology and second language learning*. London: Edward Arnold.

Gardner, R., and W. E. Lambert. 1972. *Attitudes and motivation in second language learning*. Rowley, MA: Newbury House.

Gass, S. 1988. "Integrating research areas: A framework for second language studies." *Applied Linguistics* 9: 198–217.

González, A. 1999. "Tying teacher pay, performance could boost entire profession." *USA Today* (June 18): A25.

Goodman, K. 1986. *What's whole in whole language*. Porstmouth, NH: Heinemann Educational Books.

Goswami, D., and P. R. Stillman (eds.). 1987. *Reclaiming the classroom: Teacher research as an agency for change*. Upper Montclair, NJ: Boynton/Cook. ED 277022 (not available from EDRS).

Guntermann, G. (ed.). 1993. *Developing language teachers for a changing world*. The ACTFL Foreign Language Education Series. Lincolnwood, IL: National Textbook Company.

Hammadou, J. A. 1993. "Inquiry in language teacher education." In G. Guntermann (ed.), *Developing language teachers for a changing world* (pp. 76–104). The ACTFL Foreign Language Education Series. Lincolnwood, IL: National Textbook Company.

Hammadou, J., and E. B. Bernhardt. 1987. "On being and becoming a foreign language teacher." *Theory into Practice* 26: 301–6.

Harley, B., P. Allen, J. Cummins, and M. Swain (eds.). 1990. *The development of second language proficiency*. Cambridge, England: Cambridge University Press.

Hatch, E. 1983. "Simplified input and second language acquisition." In R. W. Andersen (ed.), *Pidginization and creolization as language acquisition* (pp. 64–88). Rowley, MA: Newbury House.

Heilenman L., and I. M. Kaplan. 1985. "Proficiency in practice: The foreign language curriculum." In C. J. James (ed.), *Foreign language proficiency in the classroom and beyond*. Lincolnwood, IL: National Textbook Company.

Hiple, D. V. 1987. "A progress report on the ACTFL proficiency guidelines, 1982–1986." In H. Byrnes and M. Canale (eds.), *Defining and developing proficiency: Guidelines, implementations, and concepts* (pp. 5–24). The ACTFL Foreign Language Education Series. Lincolnwood, IL: National Textbook Company.

James, C. J. 1985. "Learning from proficiency: The unifying principle." In C. J. James (ed.), *Foreign language proficiency in the classroom and beyond* (pp. 1–8). Lincolnwood, IL: National Textbook Company.

Johnson, B. 1993. "Teacher-as-researcher." *ERIC Digest* 92–97. Washington, DC: ERIC Clearinghouse on Teacher Education. ED355205.

Kramsh, C. 1993. *Context and culture in language teaching*. Oxford, England: Oxford University Press.

Krashen, S. D. 1985. *The input hypothesis*. London: Longman.

Krashen, S. D. 1987. *Principles and practice in second language acquisition*. Englewood Cliffs, NJ: Prentice Hall.

Larsen-Freeman, D. 1985. "State of the art in second language acquisition." In S. M. Gass and C. G. Madden (eds.), *Input in second language acquisition* (pp. 433–44). Rowley, MA: Newbury House.

Larsen-Freeman, D., and M. H. Long. 1991. *An introduction to second language acquisition research*. London: Longman.

Lee, J. F. 1987. "Morphological factors influencing pronominal reference assignment by learners of Spanish; dedicated to Joseph H. Matluck." In T. A. Morgan, J. F. Lee, and B. VanPatten (eds.), *Language and language use: Studies in Spanish* (pp. 221–32). Lanham, MD: University Press of America.

Lee, J. F., and B. VanPatten. 1995. *Making communicative language teaching happen.* New York: McGraw-Hill.

Lieberman, A. 1986. "Collaborative research: Working with, not working on . . ." *Educational Leadership* 43: 28–32.

Lightbown, P. 1983. "Exploring relationships between development and instructional sequences in L2 acquisition." In H. W. Slinger and M. H. Long (eds.), *Classroom oriented research in second language acquisition* (pp. 217–44). Rowley, MA: Newbury House.

Lightbown, P. 1985. "Great expectations: Second language acquisition research and classroom teaching." *Applied Linguistics* 6: 173–89.

LoCoco, V. 1987. "Learner comprehension of oral and written sentences in German and Spanish: The importance of word order." In B. VanPatten, T. Dvorak, and J. F. Lee (eds.), *Foreign language learning: A research perspective* (pp. 119–29). Cambridge, MA: Newbury House.

Long, M. H. 1991. "Focus on form: A design feature in language teaching methodology." In K. de Bot, R. B. Ginsberg, and C. Kramsh (eds.), *Foreign language research in cross-cultural perspective* (pp. 39–53). Amsterdam/Philadelphia, PA: Benjamins.

Long, S. S. 2000. " 'Visions' of K–12 foreign language teacher recruitment in higher education." *Foreign Language Annals* 33 (4): 433–37.

McLaughlin, B. 1990. "Restructuring." *Applied Linguistics* 11: 113–28.

Miller, D. M., and G. J. Pine. 1990. "Advancing professional inquiry for educational improvement through action research." *Journal of Staff Development* 13 (3): 56–61. EJ430617.

National Standards in Foreign Language Education Project. 1996. *Standards for foreign language learning: Preparing for the 21st century.* Yonkers, NY: Author.

Nerenz, A. 1993. "Becoming a Teacher in the 21st Century." In J. K. Phillips (ed.), *Reflecting on proficiency from the classroom perspective* (pp. 161–203). Lincolnwood, IL: National Teachers Council.

Nixon, J. 1989. "The teacher as researcher: Contradictions and continuities." *Peabody Journal of Education* 64 (2): 20–32. EJ395998.

Oja, S. N., and G. J. Pine. 1983. *A two-year study of teacher stage of development in relation to collaborative action research in schools.* Durham: University of New Hampshire, Collaborative Action Research Project Office.

Omaggio Hadley, A. 1993. *Teaching language in context.* Boston, MA: Heinle & Heinle.

Ruiz-Funes, M., in collaboration with S. Henning, M. Bassman, S. Briley, and A. Borisoff-Rodgers. Forthcoming. "Eastern North Carolina high to college articulation project." *Modern Language Association/ ADFL.*

Savignon, S. J. 1972. *Communicative competence: An experiment in foreign language teaching.* Philadelphia, PA: Center for Curriculum Development.

Savignon. S. J. 1997. *Communicative competence: Theory and practice.* New York: McGraw-Hill.

Schmidt, R. 1990. "The role of consciousness in second language learning." *Applied Linguistics* 11: 129–58.

Schulz, R. 1998. "Foreign language education in the United States: Trends and challenges." *The ERIC Review* 6 (1): 6–13.

Schwartz, B. 1993. "On explicit and negative data effecting and affecting competence and linguistic behavior." *Studies in Second Language Acquisition* 15: 147–63.

Shockley, R., and L. Sevier. 1991. "Behavior management in the classroom for maintaining control." *Schools in the Middle* 1 (2): 14–18.

Shrum, J. L., and E. W. Glisan. 1994. *Teacher's handbook: Contextualized language instruction.* Boston, MA: Heinle & Heinle.

Shrum, J. L., and E. W. Glisan. 2000. *Teacher's handbook: Contextualized language instruction,* 2d ed. Boston, MA: Heinle & Heinle.

Simon, P. 1980. *The tongue-tied American.* New York: Continuum.

Spada, N. 1986. "The interaction between type of contact and type of instruction: Some effects on the L2 proficiency of adult learners." *Studies in Second Language Acquisition* 8: 181–200.

Street, L. 1986. "Mathematics, teachers, and an action research course." In D. Hustler, T. Cassidy, and T. Cuff (eds.), *Action research in classrooms and schools.* London: Allen and Unwin.

"Strength through wisdom: A critique of U.S. capability." November 1979. A report to the President from the President's Commission on Foreign Language and International Studies. *Modern Language Journal* 64 (1): 9–57.

Sullivan, J. F. 1983. "Kean offers plans to improve education." *New York Times* (September 7): II, 5.

Terrell, T. 1982. "The natural approach to language teaching: An update." *Modern Language Journal* 66: 121–32.

Terrell, T. D. 1991. "The role of grammar instruction in a communicative approach." *Modern Language Journal* 75: 52–63.

Tikunoff, W. J., and B. A. Ward. 1983. "Collaborative research in teaching." *Elementary School Journal* 83: 453–68.

VanPatten, B. 1984. "Learners' comprehension of clitic pronouns: More evidence for a word order strategy." *Hispanic Linguistics* 1: 57–67.

VanPatten, B. 1986. "Second language acquisition research and the learning/teaching of Spanish: Some research findings and their implications." *Hispania* 69: 202–16.

VanPatten, B. 1990. "The acquisition of clitic pronouns in Spanish: Two case studies." In B. VanPatten and J. F. Lee (eds.), *Second language acquisition/foreign language learning* (pp. 118–39). Clevedon, England: Multilingual Matters.

VanPatten, B. 1995. "Cognitive aspects of input processing in second language acquisition." In P. Heshemipour, I. Maldonado, and M. van Naerssen (eds.), *Festschrift for Tracy Terrell* (pp. 170–83). New York: McGraw-Hill.

VanPatten, B. 1996. *Input processing and grammar instruction in second language acquisition*. Norwood, NJ: Ablex.

VanPatten, B., and T. Cadierno. 1993. "Explicit instruction and input processing." *Studies in Second Language Acquisition* 15: 225–43.

VanPatten, B., and C. Sanz. 1995. "From input to output: Processing instruction and communicative tasks." In F. Eckman, D. Highland, P. W. Lee, J. Mileham, and R. Weber (eds.), *Second language acquisition and pedagogy*. Hillsdale, NJ: Erlbaum.

Walz, J. 1989. "Contex and contextualized language practice in foreign language teaching." *Modern Language Journal* 73: 160–68.

White, L. 1989. *Universal grammar and second language acquisition*. Amsterdam/Philadelphia, PA: Benjamins.

Williamson, K. M. 1992. "Relevance or rigor—A case for teacher as researcher." *Journal of Physical Education, Recreation and Dance* 63 (9): 17–21. EJ461928.

Wing, B. H. 1993. "The pedagogical imperative in foreign language teacher education." In G. Guntermann (ed.), *Developing language teachers for a changing world* (pp. 159–86). The ACTFL Foreign Language Education Series. Lincolnwood, IL: National Textbook Company.

Woods, P. 1983. *Sociology and the school: An interactionist viewpoint*. London: Routledge and Kegan Paul.

Zdenek, J. W. 1989. "Oral testing in the high school classroom: Helpful hints." *Hispania* 72 (3): 743–45.

Zéphir, F. 2000. "Focus on form and meaning: Perspectives of developing teachers and action-based research." *Foreign Language Annals* 3 (1): 19–30.

Index

About the Author

MARCELA T. RUIZ-FUNES is Associate Professor of Foreign Languages and Literatures, East Carolina University, Greenville, North Carolina.